Oldfield

A Community of Enslaved and Free People on Maryland's Underground Railroad

KEESHA HA

Oldfield

Oldfield

A Community of Enslaved
and Free People on Maryland's
Underground Railroad

KEESHA HA

Baltimore Heritage Press
San Diego, CA

To: Shu-Ron R. Edmonds

who joined the ancestors way too soon

*"If you make a man think that he is justly an outcast,
you do not have to order him to the back door.
He will go without being told; and if there is no back door,
his very nature will demand one."*

—Carter G. Woodson, *The Mis-Education of the Negro,* 1933

Table of Contents

Introduction

For better or worse, I carry Baltimore wherever I go. It is in my gait and in my intonation. It is how I discern people's intentions and how I navigate unfamiliar spaces. The impact of a centuries-long robust slave economy is palpable in every social, business, political, economic, religious, and especially educational experience that helped shape my identity. It was felt by both my parents and all four of my grandparents. My first breath was in a racially segregated hospital in West Baltimore at the height of the nation's Civil Rights Movement.

It was not until the birth of my son that I searched for the keys to his survival in a land that was not meant for him. The answer was with the ancestors; my genealogy journey began. My father told me that our people are from Leonardtown in St. Mary's County. He meant, of course, his father's people, which left my grandmother's heritage an afterthought. "Surviving was no mystery," he quipped, "like breathing, it's not something you think about, it's something you just do." And have lots of children, he advised.

With prodding, my father then told me that his mother's people were from Princess Anne in Somerset County (the site of the state's last documented lynching). Again, via the lens of patriarchy, he meant her father's people, which left my grandmother's mother's life a mystery.

My father had eight children. His parents, John and Calvert (née Waters) Wiley, had eleven children. Grandma Calvert, whom I had only met once, was one of thirteen born to Lillie (née Plater) and Greenwood Waters. The process of building my DNA connection to my grandparents has helped heal wounds expressed in Mahalia Jackson's rendition of the old spiritual: "Sometimes I feel like a motherless child, Sometimes I feel like I'm almost done."

Maryland has been my father's family's only home since arriving on its shores in chains from Africa—and the living has never been easy. There is very little in local and state archives or historical societies that validate the existence of relatives even one or two generations removed from my father.

The joke in "Smalltimore" is that everyone you meet is a cousin. Cousinship is more likely than not if your roots extend to Maryland's Eastern Shore. In Dorchester County, especially, everyone has a story on how they are related to Harriet Tubman–a spectacular feat considering she reportedly had no children of her own.

For all the sons, daughters, uncles, and aunts who once felt like a motherless child, this is our healing story. We are all the children that Harriet delivered.

For the ones who did not make it.

Keesha Ha
The daughter of John Wiley
The granddaughter of Calvert Waters
The great granddaughter of Lillie Plater
The 2nd great-granddaughter of Louisa Keene
The 3rd great-granddaughter of Rachel "Mother" Plater

"Liberty held to be the natural condition for other men, has been denied to the blacks... The time has arrived when this principle of exclusion should be abandoned by the State of Maryland."

Frederick Douglass, Speech, "A Friendly Word to Maryland"
Baltimore, Maryland November 17, 1864

Top (L to R) Rev. William David Vaughn Jr. (c. 1900), courtesy of the family
Winfield Ross Sr. (c.1975), courtesy of OFCCCIA
Birstal Ross (c.1960), courtesy of OFCCCIA
William Jarmon (May 2024), courtesy of OFCCCIA
Clarence Vaughn and Linda Jones. September 18, 2009, courtesy of Dorchester Star newspaper
Leven Bryan (c.1990), courtesy of the family.

"All water has a perfect memory and is forever trying to get back to where it was."

Nobel Prize Novelist Toni Morrison, 1996

Top (L to R): Mary R. Woolford (c. 1970), Louis Woolford (c. 1945), Ethel Dean (c. 1960), Mildred Moore (c. 1940), Rachel Payne (c. 1955); Gordon Stills (c. 1978). All photos courtesy of Ancestry.com..

"[O]ne of the most vital ways we sustain ourselves is by building communities of resistance, places where we know we are not alone."

–bell hooks, Yearning: Race, Gender, and Cultural Politics, 2014.

The children of Alexander and Louisa Plater at the 1936 funeral of their sister Wilhemenia Henry. Along with her siblings, Willie's survivors were her husband Jason, ten children and twenty-three grandchildren. She and her husband are buried in Oldfield Cemetery. Front: Rachel Payne. 2nd Row (L to R) Drucilla Robinson, Bertha Cummings, Olive Waters, Palestine Plater, Robert Cummings, and Palestine's wife Martha. Not shown sisters Lillie Waters and Alexzena Purnell.

The grandson of Rev. Charles and Lucinda Keene, Walter Raleigh Dean Sr (left), wife Ruth and children Annette, Patricia, Ransom, Delores, Sonia, Gloria, and Janice. Baltimore (c. 1958). Photo credit: I. Henry Phillips III.

Chapter 1

The Power of Storytelling

If Harriet Tubman did not actually exist, someone white would have surely invented tales of her exploits in fantastical fables to explain away the resilience, intuition, and determination often displayed by Black women.

It was not necessary to concoct a gargantuan blue ox or an embedded sword that only she could remove from a stone to lift the famed nurse, spy, and scout to legendary status. Known as the "Moses of her People," Tubman (c 1822-1913) birthed the Black self-liberation movement in Maryland, even though she was not known to have had children of her own to carry her legacy. Each chapter of Tubman's self-liberation exploits on Maryland's Eastern Shore is legendary beyond the imagination of any of Aesop's fables.

There is a main character in every family history story. Start the journey with a person whose life's arc spans milestones. Featured on this book's cover photo, family matriarch Mother Plater was born Rachel Farrow circa 1825 and would have been about the same age as Tubman (about 25 years old) when Tubman fled Dorchester County for the first time.

A stone's throw from Harriet Tubman's birthplace of Tobacco Stick, MD, descendants of both free and formerly enslaved people with African heritage gather annually to maintain the ancestral homeland known as Oldfield (or Old Field).

The Oldfield name has a rich provenance. The ecological term *oldfield* (sometimes *old field* or *oldfields*) refers to abandoned agricultural lands where the soil is devoid of nutrients. Only the hardiest of plants remain. Communities such as Sheppard's Old Fields in St. Mary's County and Clark's Old Fields in Harford County share the name.

Donning fancy hats and carrying the stories of ancestors, dozens of annual gatherings on Maryland's Eastern Shore keep alive the nation's earliest Black settlements. Even with such a rich history, history books in schools have selective memory. Outside of academia, even publicly funded archives are largely exclusionary towards the Black experience.

Along with caretaking, descendant communities are also responsible for elevating the recognition of places that hold both heartache and inspiration. Rakes, mortar, and remembrances are essential tools to prevent these communities from disappearing in the annals of history.

Similarly, in nearby Talbot County, the birthplace of Frederick Douglass, Unionville is believed to be the nation's only community settled by returning Black soldiers who were previously enslaved.[1] Unlike Oldfield, there is a historical marker at the cemetery next to St. Stephens A.M.E. Church. At its height, Unionville had over 40 commercial buildings, and its population is estimated today to be around 4,000.[2]

The intentionality behind Black family reunions includes committing to memory both relationships and significant events. The reexamination process reinforces shared values that, in turn, cultivate the community's identity. Above all else, the annual return to Oldfield solidifies people's dedication to service and principles of the Christian faith.

Keepers of elements of Black peoples' stories include family reunions, oral history, Bible entries, land deeds, census data, birth and death certificates, military records, newspapers, and documents from churches, cemeteries, and local archives. More recently, DNA has connected lost family members. Recent strides towards inclusion of Black communities as relevant areas for archaeological study has led to the discovery of important artifacts in the Blackwater region.

More often than not, it is the collective memory that determines a family's origin story. Those engaged in genealogy look for famous names, key battles, inventions, newsworthy events, or specific locations in order to determine their ancestral homes.

Women's origin stories are often lost when they give up their names for marriage. Within these pages, there is an intentional effort to confront the colonialist patriarchy by providing the surnames of women prior to marriage.

Black women's roles are exemplified by the historical leadership of three women of Oldfield: former Beverly School students Mary Rachel (née Henry) Woolford, Birstal (née Keene) Ross, and Ethel (née Keene) Dean of the OFCCCIA. Additionally, as national historical people of significance, two daughters of Dorchester County are amplified, Harriet Tubman and Gloria Richardson.

Recast as minor instead of central characters are the efforts of the white schoolteacher Mary S. Osbourne (sometimes spelled Osborne or Osbourn), who arrived shortly after emancipation, and of the white merchant Daniel T. Orem, who sold Black residents the land where they built their institutions. Both of their contributions are included here but framed to depict their explicit and implicit bias and prejudice as a product of their time.

While claiming cousinship to Harriet is justifiably a point of pride, the most consequential relationship to Tubman is the one Oldfield has with her grandnephew, Harkless Bowley. Bowley was born in Canada after Tubman assisted his mother to self-liberation. After emancipation, young Bowley and his parents, John and Kessiah (Kizziah is a variation), returned to their ancestral home. They purchased land adjacent to a small settlement known as Oldfield. The Bowleys later sold a tract of land that expanded Oldfield and made landowners out of people who were themselves previously owned.

The Plot Twist of the Underground Railroad

One only has to read how newspapers portrayed Harriet Tubman with a dowdy physical description and claimed ear assaults from her regional language and lack of formal education to understand the full range of her superpower. Navigating the swampy terrain as often and successfully as the tiny woman with faulty eyesight did was the plot twist no one saw coming.

The quest for freedom by those enslaved did not begin with the twenty-something-year-old's decision to leave Maryland in 1849. Movement along the Underground Railroad (UGRR) existed before Harriet Tubman was even born. Maryland, as a border state with the largest per capita number of free Black people and the largest number of successful self-liberated occurrences, was an important waystation on the way to freedom.

Oldfield was one of several villages in the swampy region of Blackwater that Harriet Tubman undoubtedly visited as she conducted travelers on the UGRR in the decade preceding the Civil War. Throughout these trips, she assuredly depended on the discretion and aid of one of her people's earliest institutions, the Oldfield Church, three miles from her home. Oldfield's origin date has not been established, but free and enslaved people worked and lived in close proximity for generations before Tubman was born.[3]

Although Tobacco Stick's name was changed to Madison after the Civil War, Oldfield has maintained not just its name but its identity and culture. As early as 1800, known Oldfield residents such as Denwood Clash, John Henry, Enoch Hughes, Matthew Pinder, William Manokey, James Stanley, and Mahalia and her son John Clash are listed as free Black people in either census or manumission papers.

History has not preserved the names of many of those who aided abolitionists or self-emancipators like Tubman. Even with the passing of decades and a century, the disclosure of individual names could be met with repercussions for their families.[4]

Luckily, an invaluable and credible source validates the brazen exploits of Tubman and other self-emancipators. Had it not been for Philadelphia-based abolitionist William Still, who kept a diary of the people he interviewed once they arrived north, the coordinated clandestine efforts that yielded multiple successful escapes would have assuredly been contradicted in the annals as African folklore.

In his 1872 book, Still revealed Black churches' crawl spaces, like that of Oldfield's, were common hiding places. Additionally, people were stealthily placed under floorboards in barns as well as inside secret wagon compartments as they sought freedom from the atrocities of slavery and human trafficking. William Still took care not to divulge the exact location or specific names of those who aided freedom seekers as they passed through Dorchester County.[5]

The village's longevity is largely due to three distinct institutions that anchored the community: a church, a school, and a private-lending entity. Oldfield's church served as its school prior to the war, and it was rebuilt in 1894 and named in honor of William D. Vaughn Sr.

Located on Old Field Road in Church Creek (previously known as Williams New Road), the historic Methodist Episcopal church is one of the oldest in the county. The adjacent Oldfield cemetery holds the gravestones of Civil War veterans, both those born free and those formerly enslaved.

In a current state of disrepair, Vaughn Chapel is closed to visitors, and the first school in the county for Black students was demolished sometime after the 1950s. Over the years, the school was known as "Beverly Institute of Free Blacks," "Oldfield School," "Oldfields," and "Colored School No. 1."[6] See Chart 6 in the Appendix for list of known Civil War veterans.

A Dorchester County Historical Society's driving tour directs visitors to two locations on Old Field Road in Church Creek: the building that was originally named Vaughn Methodist Episcopal Church at the address 2061 Old Field Rd in Church Creek and the vacant site across the road where Beverly School once stood. Both institutions served as the bedrock upon which an ancestral home was built.[7]

A member of the Vaughn, Bryan, Cornish and Chester family, Leon Harris, recalls working the farm, going to Vaughn M.E. church, walking a mile to the nearest store, and visiting his cousins on Egypt Road while visiting his grandmother Sinia (née Bryan) Harris in the 1960s. Upon learning that his ancestral home on the one-and-a-half-acre lot that bordered the cemetery and was last owned by his great-grandparents William L. and Elizabeth (née Chester) Bryan in 2009 was taken by the county for unpaid taxes, the 78-year-old Baltimorean was deflated that he could never go home again.[8]

In addition to Vaughn Chapel church, Oldfield is also notable for having the first school for Black people in the county. In a Bureau of Refugees, Freedmen, and Abandoned Lands report (commonly referred to as "Freedmen's Bureau") report from Mary S. Osbourne, a white teacher who arrived from Massachusetts in 1865, she notes that the Black residents of Oldfield paid for and built the county's first school for Black students when the Civil War ended. Residents named it Beverly School in honor of the New England town that sponsored Osbourne's tenure as teacher. After her departure, a Black farmer from nearby Tobacco Stick, John H. Keene, assumed leadership of the school's mission to educate future educators.[9]

Many people within and outside the community have helped shape and sustain Oldfield. Some names have been amplified in the historical record, some muted, and others simply forgotten. Surnames commonly associated with Oldfield's founding and expansion include Banks, Bryan, Camper, Cephas, Chester, Clash, Cornish, Dixon, Ennals, Henry, Hill, Hughes, Jackson, Jarmon, Jolley, Kane, Keene, Kiah, Macer, Manokey, Marine, Pinder, Plater, Ross, Stanley, Stiles, and Woolford.

Without the service of Civil War veterans such as James Dixon, John Fisher, and brothers Alexander and William Hughes, the story of Oldfield might have faded from historical significance. Those who returned (or their survivors) used their government pensions and bounty payments to help grow and nourish Oldfield.

Just as it was at its origin, volunteer labor is foundational to the preservation of Oldfield. The Old Field Church Creek Community Improvement Association (OFCCCIA) is responsible for the upkeep of the remaining building structures, and volunteers maintain the old cemetery. With faith and perseverance, they turned the tide— transforming from once being owned to becoming owners of the land they farmed.

The generation that benefited from the 19th-century church and school, in turn, created an economic system known as the Beverly United Stock Club in the early 20th century. The charter document for Oldfield's version of Black Wall Street details how elders pooled their money to finance loans and mortgages over decades. The pillars of ingenuity and self-determination continue to combat oppressive, systemic racism in financial institutions, all while instilling values of faith, service, and community for families in the small village on Maryland's Eastern Shore.[10]

What is today considered sacred ground once included not just the church and school, but also a general store and multiple farms, populated by close-knit neighbors. The number of residents has diminished along with the acreage, but generational land ownership and the dedication of descendants have ensured Oldfield's continued relevance.

Just as people are discarded, so it is with places. When circumstances are unfavorable to the oppressors, colonizers, and conquerors, such erasure is common. Not much has been preserved to document the lived experiences of the Indigenous peoples or the enslaved Africans who grew strong from the bounty provided by the Choptank and Nanticoke Rivers. Despite efforts to dam the stream of Oldfield's history, it finds a way to reach those willing to receive it.

Oldfield Church, rebuilt in 1894 and renamed Vaughn Methodist Episcopal, with cornerstone superimposed. Currently known as Vaughn Chapel. (2019) Credit: Keesha Ha

Chapter 2

Memories and Memorials

With elements of both art and science, genealogy weaves the two together to arrive at truths. Just as memories fade, people's perspectives can be trusted only as far as their attachment to their realities takes them. When facts are the goal, it can be a pursuit fraught with inconsistencies.

Luckily, faded newspapers provide a glimpse into the lives of people who lived on the margins outside of Church Creek, near Cambridge on Maryland's Eastern Shore. There is no marker to commemorate the lives of the people of Oldfield or map coordinates to direct people to the location.

Memories fade faster than ink, but the staying power of personal photographs are constant reminders of those who left. However, digitized historical newspapers are a great genealogical resource because they capture snapshots of a moment in time, especially deaths, births, marriages, and legal events such as land transfers and criminal court proceedings. Since 1892 the *Baltimore Afro-American* published "in the interest of the race" opinions and events that shaped the culture and became a time capsule of Black history.

The community's unofficial newspaper of record, "The Afro" commemorated the eighty-sixth birthday in 1960 of Elizabeth (née Chester) Bryan, the widow of William L. Bryan (1854-1931). The birthday girl was celebrated with a photo in the paper, an image not seen by her great, great granddaughter Dina Wiley Payne, nor her great grandson Leon Harris before viewing the newspaper clipping in 2025.[11]

Mother Plater's name made it in the newspaper when she was about 90 years old. Over the course of her lifespan, which is estimated to be 110 years, census records show that at various times she lived in the household with her grandchildren and great-grandchildren.[12]

For several years old Santa Claus has brought much happiness to Aunt Rachel Plater, an old colored woman who is very nearly .if not quite, a hundred years old. She has been "Aunt Rachel" in this community for a great many years; in fact, some of the older citizens state that she was a middle-aged woman when they were children. "Aunt Rachel" lives at No. 7 Fairmount avenue, and, like a child, she looks forward with much eagerness to the Christmas season.

L to R: Newspaper clipping showing Mother Rachel referred to as "Aunt Rachel." Courtesy of The Daily Banner newspaper, Cambridge, MD. December 21, 1918. Dina Wiley Payne and her 98-year old grandmother Elizabeth "Sis" Stewart. 2025. Credit: Dina Wiley Payne.

Newspapers mentioned Oldfield, mostly in obituaries that were submitted by family members or in announcements about school or religious events. In 1896, the Baltimore Sun newspaper included "Ole Field" in its profile of Black settlements in an article, *Negro Villages Self-Taught and Progressive Colored People of Dorchester County*. Also mentioned were Harrisville (the location of Malone Cemetery), Smithsville, Gun Swamp, and Christ Rock. The most favorable description was of "Ole

Field" rechristened Beverly as "a most orderly and attractive-looking place of residence for prosperous colored folk."[13]

Cambridge's *Daily Banner* newspaper took notice in 2007, when former Boston Red Sox's 1995 American League MVP Maurice "Mo" Vaughn returned to his ancestral home.[14] Vaughn's father, Dr. Leroy S. Vaughn, brought his children to his ancestral home on the Maryland Eastern Shore for the annual Heritage Weekend. The former three-time All-Star's grandfather, Samuel Kiah Vaughn (1910-56), is the grandnephew of the church's namesake.

The Major League baseball star does not have any paternal cousins and recalls family reunions to visit his maternal cousins, aunts and uncles in Virginia. Mo had never been to the Eastern Shore, and it was a culture shock. The invitation came at a time when Mo was intentionally placing value on things in life that previously the demands of professional sports did not often permit.[15]

Indigenous Peoples

One must rely primarily on storytelling to connect Mother Plater to the Indigenous people who predate British colonialism. Newspapers' society pages and legal notices are not useful sources to amplify the lives of Native People.

Church Creek sits along Route 16, which follows a Native American trail used for seasonal migration and trade between the Chesapeake and Delaware Bays that dates to pre-Colonial days. The tribal culture familiar to those of us with African and Native ancestry aided us historically to live harmoniously, combining wisdom, culture, and ultimately bloodlines on what has become government-owned property.

Not surprisingly, data that could aid Native American genealogy is scant, especially in community and national newspapers. Maryland recognized the Piscataway tribe in 2012, and there are no federally recognized tribes. FamilySearch.org, the database maintained by the

Church of Jesus Christ of Latter-Day Saints (LDS), has links for a variety of repositories.

Had it not been for the Native peoples of the Americas, who generously assisted Europeans with food, shelter, and hunting education, their expedition would have concluded in mass deaths. In turn, the British colonizers moved to conquer the native dwellers of Virginia and Maryland. For the next 150 years, while the transatlantic slave trade was legal, Europeans (initially the Portuguese and Spanish and later the British) captured and brought by force people of African descent across the Atlantic to the Americas. As they prospered economically, colonial Marylanders proposed treaties to usurp land from the Indigenous people of the Choptank and Nanticoke.

Native Americans were systematically forced off their land where they lived for thousands of years while the slave trade expanded. These marginalized groups created their own communities that included intermarrying. Not only are archival systems lax in documenting treaty violations against Native Americans, but descendants have been distanced from both their African and Native American tribal roots and culture.

Buildings and documents can be destroyed, but stories last as long as there is someone to tell them.

Chapter 3

Roots Wide and Deep

If surviving is considered an act of resistance, then memorializing the struggle is the epitome of perseverance. Holding space for Church Creek's little-known Black community to regain its relevance has been a generational responsibility.

One cannot pursue the history of Black families without accessing the depth of institutional knowledge sacredly held within Black churches. Perusing the hallowed halls of Historically Black Colleges and Universities (HBCUs) for dissertations, yearbooks, books, journals, and private collections will reveal the breadth of the struggle. The most solemn reminder of those who dedicated their lives to carve out a place in this county is etched on the headstones of graves in any of this nation's Black-only cemeteries.[16]

Two of Oldfield's native sons are widely credited for their visionary organizational leadership in preserving the community's institutional history: Winfield Ross Sr. (1893-1984) and WWII veteran Alfred Henry Sr. (1909-95).

Ross founded the Old Field Church Creek Community Improvement Association (OFCCCIA), the legal entity that serves as the fundraising and preservation arm for the community. Henry Sr. organized the

Memorial Day service at the historic church and cemetery that functioned at times like a family reunion.[17]

In 1956, Ross implemented OFCCCIA in response to the growing difficulty of maintaining the cemetery, the church, and the school (by then in great disrepair) as people relocated to other areas. Descendants had always been responsible for funding repairs, maintenance, and construction of Oldfield's structures and land, and while they were dedicated to the community's upkeep, it was becoming too difficult to manage for the aging population.

While Ross did not have military experience, he registered for the WWI draft. Ross shares the same surname as world-renowned patriot Harriet (née Ross) Tubman, but no familial connection has been made. Winfield was raised by his uncle, Alexander Ross Sr., and his wife, Birstal (Keene) Ross. It is likely that Winfield's mother was Alexander's sister, Susan J. Ross, and his paternity is not a part of his record.[18]

Henry Sr., another native son and about 10 years younger than Ross, inspired families to return to Oldfield each Memorial Day to recognize the community's military veterans. For what began in the 1950s and has been maintained every year since, the longevity likely would have been seen as a great honor for the son of Joseph and Melvina (nee McGlotten) Henry.[19]

Henry Sr. enlisted into the Army at age thirty-five at Camp Lee, VA. After the war, he worked at a local cannery while his wife, Claretta, worked as a schoolteacher at Beverly as well as other racially segregated schools. Henry Sr. retired after years of working at a dry cleaner's in Cambridge. The Henry family attended Bethel A.M.E. Church in Cambridge.[20]

Each Sunday prior to Memorial Day, people continue to gather from across states and oceans to honor those from Oldfield who served in this nation's armed forces. Importantly, these events offer visibility for the patriotic devotion of Black men who, with tenuous citizenship, remain marginalized as veterans of foreign wars. While significantly overrepresented in this country's military (both historically and today), the opportunity to serve honorably remains heralded by those connected to the Oldfield community.[21]

The Association's Baltimore Branch

Even as residency in Church Creek dwindled, membership in the association grew in large part due to the efforts of Winfield Ross and his wife, Mary (née Bryan). The combined Ross and Bryan families were instrumental in establishing a committee based in Baltimore, where the couple raised their three children. The majority of Mary's ten siblings also relocated to Baltimore and were active in the Association.

During the 1950s, Ross and Bryan's extended families were integral in the process and planning of Oldfield's most recent building, a community hall to accommodate the pilgrimage by out-of-towners to Oldfield – mainly from Baltimore, Philadelphia, and Cape May, NJ. When it was time for construction, it took the entire village: Emerson Bryan (Winfield's brother-in-law), Fred Chester, Jason Henry, Clifton Plater, Clarence Vaughn, John Vaughn, William "David" Vaughn, and Rev. Wilbert Woolford carried the lion's share. In 1994, the building was renamed *Ross Hall* in his honor. Both the Ross and Bryan families have Oldfield Cemetery plots.

In 1974, with Ross as its president, the association acquired ownership of the church and hall's land. The church had been placed on limited-service status by what was then named the Peninsula Conference of the United Methodist Church due to declining church attendance. Once removed from its auspices, the church became known simply as Vaughn Chapel.[22]

The continued growth of the Baltimore branch of the association can be attributed to cousins Birstal (née Keene) Ross and Ethel (née Keene) Dean of that city.[23] Birstal (1895-1963) was the daughter of Beverly School's first Black teacher, John H. Keene of nearby Tobacco Stick. Her cousin Ethel (1889-1963) was the daughter of a different John Keene, who was one of fourteen children born to Rev. Charles and Lucinda (née Henry) Keene of Oldfield. As contemporaries and both highly respected, the two John Keenes are distant cousins, likely sharing a 2nd or 3rd great-grandparent.

Past association presidents William "David" Vaughn (1901–80), Leven Bryan (1907–99), and Clarence E. Vaughn Jr. (1929–2019) each left an indelible mark as leaders of the association. David Vaughn is the grandson of the man for whom the church is named. Under Leven Bryan's leadership, the land ownership for Vaughn Chapel returned to the community. (His sister Mary is Winfield Ross's wife of the Baltimore committee).

Clarence E. Vaughn Jr., also a direct descendant of the church's namesake, began memorializing Oldfield's history in the programs for the annual gatherings. He spent his life in service to others in Baltimore and his later home in Harford County, MD, where he was the first Black man appointed to the city's Board of Appeals. A Morgan State University (HBCU) alumnus, Vaughn was active in Iota Alpha Lambda, the NAACP, Sickle Cell Anemia Foundation, Black Youth in Action, and Black Ministerial Association.

Vaughn's message as president in association events provided historical insight into Oldfield. The association's mission, "to preserve what remains of a once thriving Black community of property owners who were the sons and daughters of former slaves, freedmen and their descendants," was often repeated.[24]

In the 2005 program booklet "Our Second Heritage Weekend Celebration September 17-18, 2005," Clarence E. Vaughn Jr. offered the following remembrances:

> I remember Halloween activities at Beverly School during the month of October; bird hunting and target practice with my grandfather (Clarence Vaughn) on Mr. Emerson Bryan's farm; visits with my great-great aunt Sophia V. Henry; Mother's Day visits with Mr. Tom and cousin Ida Ross; trips to the cemetery with Aunt Sarah to visit the graves of family members; and the Vaughn recitals held at the Chapel and the church in Church

Creek. I never dreamed of becoming a member of an organization whose mission is to preserve our heritage in a community that impacted my life as a child.[25]

William Jarmon followed Clarence Vaughn's tenure and served until 2025. Jarmon (a fourth cousin to this writer) was recognized for his near-decade-long leadership at the 130th anniversary commemoration of Vaughn Chapel during the 2024 Memorial Day service at Oldfield Cemetery, which was preceded by a banquet at the Elks Club in Cambridge.

A retired teacher, Jarmon educates visitors at both the Harriet Tubman Underground Railroad Visitor Center and serves as an executive director of the Harriet Tubman Museum and Educational Center in Cambridge. Jarmon's paternal grandfather, Rickson Jarmon Jr., is a descendant of Littleton and Hester (née Atkinson) Hughes, who were among the first families of Oldfield. Jarmon's paternal grandmother, Viola (Henry) Jarmon, is a descendant of William D. Vaughn.

Women of the Association

Dr. Melissa Glee McGuire assumed the Association president position in 2025 (a third cousin to this writer). The distinction of the first woman elected goes to Mary (née Henry) Woolford (1904–2005); she also held the honorary title of president emeritus as she approached her centennial birthday.

Woolford is a first cousin twice removed from this writer. The late president emeritus is also a double cousin, as this writer is a cousin to her father, Jason Henry, in addition to her mother, Wilhemena (née Plater) Henry. She and her husband, Rev. J. Wilbert Woolford, had ten children that they raised on a farm first in Oldfield and later in Airey, MD. Her two daughters, Gloria and Rosetta, continue to be valuable oral history resources.

Since the early 2000s, Rev. Linda Jones and Calmetta (née Woolford) Brinkley have helped set the standard for future generations of women in more front-facing leadership positions. Rev. Jones pastored at St. James A.M.E. Church in Snow Hill and Mount Olive A.M.E. Church in Salisbury, both in Maryland.

A retired educator and resident of Delaware, Calmetta Brinkley has been a lifelong member of the Cambridge committee. Her dedication is representative of the organizational prowess of the women of Oldfield over generations. In addition to being a repository and disseminator of oral history, Calmetta has served as a bridge between generations.

Brinkley is a double cousin to many Oldfield residents (not uncommon, since unions between friends, neighbors, and in-laws were encouraged in this close-knit community). See Chapter Eight for how double cousins impact DNA mapping. Calmetta's parents, Louis Woolford and Arneda Vaughn, are direct descendants of two of the area's oldest families, the Vaughn/Dixon (maternal) and Henry/Plater (paternal) families.

Calmetta's late husband, Harry Brinkley, descends from noted abolitionists in Delaware who worked with Harriet Tubman to bring enslaved people to freedom. In October 2025, she represented the family during the unveiling of a state marker for the historic free black community (Brinkley Hill) in Camden, DE, just south of Dover.

Although in Zora Neale Hurston's seminal novel, *Their Eyes Were Watching God*, her character described Black women as the "mules of the world", owing to how everyone is apt to lay their burdens on their backs, Black women are not genetically superior—quiet as it is kept. Black women have honed awareness of circumstances for potential harm, combined with faith, to survive not only the Middle Passage, but every single day that followed.

The women of Oldfield were also charged with the maintenance and growth of the Black family. With determination, love, and humanity, the displaced children of Africa built a community of self-reliance out of necessity, at times in alliance with their Native American neighbors.

Chapter 4

We Shall Not Be Moved

Some call it fortitude, others gumption—but at its essence, Black people possess strength. Places of worship are often viewed as the sole safe haven for Black people seeking to build community and reinforce the family's moral center in this country. This is true, especially in the South.

People's church homes can be valuable resources to assist in building family trees if they can be obtained, but publicly available land and tax documents can easily reveal the depths of a community's roots. In addition, and on occasion, Black people left behind wills, land deeds, correspondence, publications, and other legal filings that grounded them to their community.

While in other states, research of government records prior to emancipation was futile (beyond the enslaver's last will and testament), this was not the case in the most northern of the southern states. Maryland's free population was nearly equal to its enslaved population by 1860, as displayed as Chart 1 in the Appendix.

Rev. Charles Keene, the likely pre-war administrator of Oldfield School and pastor of Oldfield church, was born free in circa 1820. In Mary S. Osbourne's first impression of him (a white teacher from the north), she described the tutelary spirit of Oldfield that Keene embodied as one of self-reliance. Her remembrances turn on its ear the trope of helpless Black men in desperate need of a white savior:

> He seems to understand the wants of his people, and told me anything I wanted done should be attended to at once, just let them know what it was. I suspect there are many teachers in New England who would be only too happy to have their patrons visit them with such a generous offer.[26]

Osbourne arrived as part of the initiative by the Bureau of Refugees, Freedmen, and Abandoned Lands (commonly referred to as "Freedmen's Bureau") that began to establish schools for formerly enslaved people. She wrote about her visit to Oldfield's church, which doubled as its school: "On Friday, Mr. Orem accompanied me on a visit to the 'colored Church,' that I might look over my ground. I found the house in as good condition as could be expected. It was clean, though the furniture was of the simplest kind; [. . .] Hard seats for little ones to occupy six hours in a day."[27]

In a few short weeks in late 1865, Dorchester County Circuit Court records show that Charles Keene purchased land that had been inherited by the family of a War of 1812 veteran to secure the future of Oldfield. See Deed 1 in the Appendix.

Despite racial prejudices embedded within religious organizations that upheld tenets of white supremacy, religious institutions remained bedrocks of the community. Even terroristic threats, such as church burnings, did not deter Vaughn's congregation from living a life of service to others. The combined spirit of family, faith, and community reached across generations and is evident in early records of Dorchester County.

The church building that exists today (named for the Vaughn family) rests on land that a veteran of the US Colored Troops (USCT), John Fisher, purchased in December 1893. Members of the Parker and Linthicum families (their history as Europeans is extensively included in the county's archives) sold the land to John Fisher (1840-1918) for seventy-five dollars (about $4,000 in today's valuation).[28] Both the Parker and Linthicum family burial plots are at Church Creek's Old Trinity Church's cemetery, a National Historic Landmark (NHL).

In a generous act of service to his community, Fisher (a farmer and local preacher) and his wife, Jane (née Cornish), sold their newly acquired land to "the Trustees of Vaughn Chapel of Beverly" for twenty-five dollars on July 4, 1894.[29] The Fishers' adopted daughter, Jessie (1890-1961), and her husband, Frederick Douglass Keene Sr. (1887-1966), are both buried at Oldfield Cemetery.[30] Their daughter, Inez (who married Roger Moore), was a leader in Baltimore's social justice movement as a member of the historic Trinity A.M.E. Church.[31] Inez died in November 2016, barely two months shy of her 102nd birthday.

Vaughn Chapel congregants became notable local preachers. A married couple who attended Vaughn, Reverends Lewis and Sarah (Cromwell) Bayneum (1885-1943), found their ministry in Cambridge's Ward 2. They are grandparents of two notable graduates of Cambridge's historical Black high school: Judge Joanne Bayneum Bowens and Pastor Alma Boulden. Rev. Lewis Bayneum (1877-1954) was also a member of the Beverly Stock Club, discussed in a later chapter.[32]

As superintendent of Sunday Schools at Knox Presbyterian Church in 1946, Baltimore's Rev. George Randolph Keene (1893-1962) was a lay leader in early childhood education before joining the ministry. Keene, a former schoolteacher and WWI veteran, is the son of the county's first Black schoolteacher, John H. Keene. The former Navy sailor's descendants are DNA matches to this writer (third cousin); like his father, he is buried at Oldfield Cemetery.[33]

The Vaughn Namesake

The cornerstone of Oldfield's second post-emancipation building, Vaughn Methodist Episcopal (ME) Church of Beverly, was set in 1894. The Vaughn surname (Vaughan as a variation) was named in honor of free villagers William and Harriet (née Lee) Vaughn's son, William D. Vaughn Sr. (1829-1905). The church's namesake and his wife, Mary Ann (née Hooper), left behind a legacy that includes their reported thirteen children who were raised in Church Creek and in the Christian faith.

Words from their daughter, Sophia, were memorialized by the newspaper dedicated to the Black community known as "The Afro." In 1959, she spoke to a reporter from the *Baltimore Afro-American* newspaper and attributed her good health and longevity to her faith on the occasion of her 91st birthday.[34]

The nonagenarian also shared memories of her parents at the church before a new one was built in 1894, named in their honor. Born on July 18, 1868, Sophia recounted her wedding day in 1885 in the parsonage of the antebellum era church, "My dress was pink [...] with wide, flowing skirts and a firm bodice." She recalled that her brother William Vaughn Jr. (1863-1901) was an AME minister and a schoolteacher in the family church.[35]

While Sophia did not state a familial relationship to Harriet Tubman, she cited three of that era's most well-known surnames, such as: Clash, Cornish, and St. Clair. Sophia and her husband, Jeremiah Henry Sr. (1873-c1945), had 13 children. A daughter, Viola Henry, married Rickson Jarmon Sr., the grandfather of local historian and educator William Jarmon.

As it is with the Clash family, Sophia's connection to Cambridge's St. Clair family is likely through marriage. Her father's sister, Harriet Vaughn, married Durham Clash (c1825-c1915); their children were her first cousins.[36]

At the time of the 1959 article's publishing, Sophia recalled having 33 grandchildren, 61 great-grandchildren, and 25 great-great-grandchildren,

Join the army of the Lord. Stay close to Him. I have been a lifelong member of the church. I never touched a drop of strong drink in my life, and I never smoked a cigarette.

– Sophia Henry

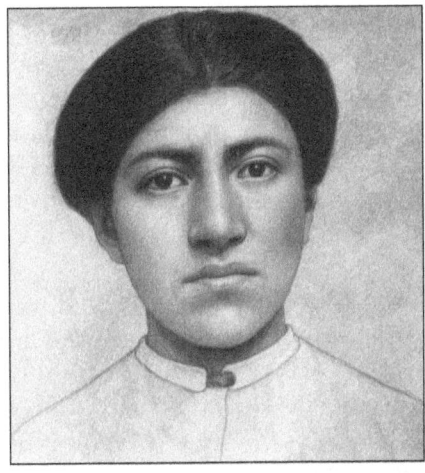

Left: Photo of Sophia Henry (1959), Courtesy of the AFRO American Newspapers Archives/Afro Charities

Above: Drawing of Sophia's paternal aunt Charity Pinder. (Circa 1870). Artist unknown. Courtesy of the family.

The church's namesake, William D. Vaughn Sr., has four known siblings: Harriet (c1830-1913), Isaac Jeremiah (c1833-unk), Charity (1835-c1880), and Benjamin (c1840-c1895). All five are included by name as free people on the 1850 census with their parents. Notably, the children of Charity and her husband Charles Pinder relocated to the New England area after emancipation for increased opportunities with the encouragement of Beverly school teacher Mary S. Osbourne.

They, along with a contingency of Hughes relatives, relocated to Rhode Island and formed a familial branch of the Oldfield descendant tree later recognized as the Pinderhughes. That branch later bore Wiley and Thomas descendants from that region.[37]

In response to the systematic familial displacement that resulted from slavery and human trafficking, the quest for reunification has been never-ending. People attempted to maintain connections across the Mason-Dixon line using newspaper ads and church announcements.

Church Recognition and Preservation

The church's name changed again in 1974, becoming simply Vaughn Chapel. This was due to declining membership, which led to its removal from under the auspices of the Methodist Episcopal Church. Because of its more central location, members of the congregation largely moved to Waugh Chapel United Methodist Church in Cambridge. At that time, the Peninsula Conference of the United Methodist Church conveyed the land to the OFCCCIA.[38]

Vaughn Chapel's centennial was celebrated at the church in May 1994, which reinvigorated the annual Memorial Day homecoming. In the fall of 2002, association president Clarence Vaughn led the inaugural Heritage Weekend dinner celebration at Dorchester Lodge; the theme was "Preserving the Heritage." In recognition of 100 years, commemorative memorials were described in the 1994 program as follows:

- a wooden cross in the pulpit was made by Maggie Green, in the name of John Fisher,
- a brass cross and candlesticks were designed by Clarence E. Vaughn and crafted by James Dawkins of Mississippi, in the name of William and Mary Vaughn
- banners for the lectern, table, and walls were made by Ruth Vaughn, in memory of Clarence and Louise Vaughn and Clarence and Sarah Cornish, and for William David and Cecelia Vaughn and their daughter, Arneda Woolford.[39]

The Heritage Weekend's printed program booklets were the first publications that collected people's first-hand knowledge of Oldfield. They documented that the timber used in building the wood-frame church was harvested from the property of members of the community. The communion table and another table used for presenting the offering were crafted specifically for the church, "hewed by artisans" who donated their time and talents.

The historical programs state that in 1925, the church was renovated; the original pump organ was too dilapidated to be salvaged, and the original silver collection plates were replaced by larger brass plates. One of the original wood-burning stoves used for heat remains in the sanctuary. The financial generosity of Mildred Henry Taylor is credited with additional improvements in the 1950s, which included the addition of a restroom and kitchen updates.[40]

In recognition of Vaughn Chapel's 130-year anniversary, Monica R. J. Bland, a Keene/Henry descendant, and Dr. Melissa Glee McGuire, a Plater/Dixon descendant, organized a May 2024 banquet held in Cambridge's Elk Lodge in cooperation with the OFCCCIA. The event's commemorative booklet includes a message from current association president William Jarmon, as well as a tribute to his predecessor, Clarence E. Vaughn.[41]

In his presidential message, William Jarmon referenced the continuing efforts to maintain the cemetery, the completion of Ross Hall renovation that started in 2023, and that plans were being considered to address the deterioration of Vaughn Chapel. "We will not let our ancestors' labor fall by the wayside," wrote Jarmon in the same program.[42]

In the program's tribute to Clarence Vaughn that extended beyond his duties as Association president, the proclamation reads in part: "Whereas Clarence E. Vaughn was approached by local families, far and near, sharing oral stories about the myths and facts surrounding Ross Hall, Old Field Cemetery and families associated with the area locals still call Kentuck Swamp (Blackwater Refuge)."[43]

Community Service Leaders and the Civil Rights Movement

Author and academic, Charles M. Payne Jr. (a Plater/Keene descendant) captured the essence of Student Nonviolent Coordinating Committee (SNCC)'s organizing in Mississippi during the Civil Rights Movement in his book, *"I've Got the Light of Freedom: The Organizing Tradition and the Mississippi Freedom Struggle"*: "People in the country might be slower to come around, but once they do, the sense of community among them makes them easier to organize[...]. Once the country people did make a commitment, it was solid."[44]

As the SNCC scholar is aware, closer to his ancestral home, women from Dorchester County claimed similar positions during the mid-20th century. A national figure in the Cambridge Movement, Gloria (née Hayes) Richardson steered Cambridge's SNCC branch. With Richardson's influence, the Cambridge Nonviolent Action Committee (CNAC) gained nationwide attention when Maryland's governor imposed martial law, which put the state's racial discord on the desk of President John F. Kennedy.

Richardson's iconic photo of her pushing aside a bayonet encapsulates the determination of a people and a time. The determined daughter of John and Mabel (née St. Clair) Hayes led meetings at Bethel AME Church during the summer of 1963.

"Promoting formal education also fell within the scope of the St. Clair family's community service. They helped establish the black school system in Cambridge and stood up for equal educational opportunities," wrote Joseph R. Fitzgerald in his biography *The Struggle is Eternal: Gloria Richardson and Black Liberation*.[45]

At its height in 1963, the Cambridge Nonviolent Action Committee (CNAC) took its cue from Richardson whose stance towards liberation was more akin to tactics later associated with the Black Panther Party that at times conflicted with the philosophy espoused Rev. Dr. Martin Luther King Jr. As King's views on non-violence were not the methods often chosen by Eastern Shore residents, his visits were eventually halted. Segregationists threw Molotov cocktails in Black neighborhoods in opposition to King, and locals responded with gunfire. It was clear that Richardson's tactics were preferred to those who understood the intricacies of Maryland's embattled history towards self-liberation.

The admiration and respect Richardson held for Malcolm X, who saw her tactics as "radical," unlike the "old guard civil rights organizations," wrote Fitzgerald. In solidarity with Richardson, Malcom X delivered his "Ballot or Bullets" speech that encouraged Black people to vote as a bloc or not at all. "[Richardson] also asked Malcom to include another warning in his speeches: if the Democratic and Republican Parties ignored black voters, black people might conclude that electoral politics had nothing to offer them, leaving them no choice but to resort to armed resistance."[46]

Extended Family Branches and their Life of Service

Native sons and daughters ventured beyond the swampy borders of Maryland's Eastern Shore to make contributions to their new communities. Descendants from the Rhode Island Hughes/Pinder family include Maya Wiley, the civil rights attorney who ran a competitive race for mayor of New York City in 2021 and is a contributor to MSNBC, along with her father, the national civil rights leader, George A. Wiley, who drowned in a 1973 Chesapeake Bay boating accident.

"[George] Wiley was born in 1931 into a middle-class Warwick, R.I. family. His family included several generations of able and ambitious people who, had their skin been white, might have been business or political leaders," wrote the *New York Times* in a 1977 article.[47]

George's brother, Judge Alton William Wiley Sr., was Rhode Island's first Black Assistant US District Attorney. Their mother, Olive (née Thomas) Wiley, was a social justice advocate and was inducted into the Rhode Island Heritage Hall of Fame in 1985 along with her husband, William Wiley. The elder Wiley was a newspaper editor and co-founder and president of the Rhode Island Urban League.

The Wiley brothers' maternal grandmother, Emily Pinder (1869-1947), was one of eight children born in Church Creek to Charity (née Vaughn), who was considered a "mulatto" and Charles A. Pinder (c1830-70), who was a named trustee on the original deed for Beverly School. Emily is buried in a family plot in Oakland Cemetery in Cranston, R.I.

The New York Times article that reviews Nick Kotz and Mary Lyn Kotz's biography on Wiley noted that the man with Oldfield roots was "one of the most important and least-known civil rights leaders of the 1960s. At a time when the Civil Rights Movement was largely middle-class in composition and in its dreams, he concentrated on the economic needs of poor blacks, founding the now defunct National Welfare Rights Organization (N.W.R.O)."[48]

Future generations can look to the past as they navigate their way forward. The spirit of family, faith, and community has its roots in the Eastern Shore, but is alive and thriving in Rhode Island, the home of the George Wiley Center. Founded in 1981, the Center continues with its mission to create social and economic change through public policy by organizing locally in Rhode Island.[49]

In later years, as part of the great migration, Plater descendants found a home in Cape May, NJ. This includes noted academic, activist, and author Charles M. Payne Jr. His father, WWII veteran Charles M. Payne Sr. (1921-92), was born in Dorchester County. In 1968, Payne Sr. was the first Black person elected to a governing body in Cape May County. Charles Sr.'s grandparents were Alexander and Louisa Plater. They are the shared ancestors of this writer, making them first cousins, twice removed.

As part of oral history, a family Inn owned and operated by Payne Sr.'s aunt Olive (née Plater) Waters (1888-1968) was included in the famed Green Book that directed Black motorists to accommodations that would likely be safe from violent race-based attacks. Relatives who traveled to New Jersey to attend "Aunt Ollie's" 70th birthday celebration in 1958 were reported by The Afro was an aid to help verify familial relationships. Attendees included Dr. Jesse Keene of Washington, D.C., Rachel (née Henry) and her husband Theodore

Stanley from New York City, as well as Wilbert and Mary Woolford from the Eastern Shore. Local family members included Ollie and her husband Archie Waters' daughter Florence (1918-96) and her husband Kenneth Stewart as well as their children Ronald, Judith, Michael, Linda, Eloise, and Christopher Stewart.[50] Charles Jr.'s uncle, James A. Plater (1912-74), a US Navy veteran, was heralded by the NAACP for innovative membership campaigns and fundraising drives for the civil rights organization on Navy vessels.

Seeking freedom as part of the migration north, many descendants who left the Eastern Shore did not leave their faith. In nearby Washington, D.C., Rev. Timothy Keene (1850-1921) and his wife, Rosa (née Cromwell) (c 1870-c 1950) were active with the A.M.E. conference. Their son, Dr. Jesse Keene (1900-70), broke color barriers at Harvard University before pursuing a prestigious career at Howard University's medical school.

Rev. and Mrs. Keene's daughter, Leona (née Keene) Lloyd, was a teacher in the Washington, DC public school system from 1915 to 1958. Both of Leona's daughters, Martha and Ruth, were educators as well. Rev. Keene is the son of Charles and Lucinda (née Henry) Keene, this author's 3rd great-grandfather, which makes Rev. Keene a 2nd great-granduncle to this writer.

Baltimore was also a destination point in the Great Migration. The Dean family pictured at the book's opening with his wife and children was captured by celebrated photographer Irving Phillips and has become symbolic of the movement. Just outside of Baltimore, Rev. William G. Bryan (1904-64) served as pastor of the historic Mt. Gilboa African Methodist Episcopal (AME) Church, built pre-war in Howard County, MD. The church served a community of enslaved and free Black people in nearby Oella.[51] His direct ancestor, Moses Hicks Chester of nearby Bucktown and a USCT veteran, married the former Joanna Hughes.[52]

Anecdotally, this writer's maternal ancestors are from a community of free Blacks in Oella and are buried at Mt. Gilboa church's cemetery. Oella is home to Benjamin Banneker (1731-1806), a Black self-taught mathematician, surveyor, astronomer, and abolitionist. A park and museum are dedicated in Banneker's honor, on 144 acres where over 28,000 artifacts have been discovered since 1979.[53]

Christian Communities

In the 1780s, Black Methodists, in protest of discrimination from the larger M.E. Church, established an independent denomination known as the African Methodist Episcopal (A.M.E) Church. In Dorchester County, despite the resistance from the white M.E. organization, Simon Brown opened a place of worship on property owned by Stephen Camper. Bethel AME Church in Cambridge was mysteriously destroyed by fire in 1877 and was rebuilt two years later. Maryland State Archives (MSA) has documents on the history of both the Stanley School and Bethel A.M.E Church in its collection.[54]

It is believed based on oral history that Oldfield's church (before it was rebuilt in 1894 and named for William D. Vaughn Sr.) predates Waugh Chapel, founded circa 1825. Destroyed by fire in 1837, Waugh was rebuilt the following year. The existing brick building was built in 1871 and has had multiple renovations since. Stephen Johns/Jones, born into slavery in 1818 oversaw the Waugh and Church Creek circuit for the Methodist Church's Delaware Conference.[55]

Today, Church Creek is without a Black church. Christ Rock M.E. Church, just like Vaughn Chapel, was once located in Church Creek. Its wood-frame building was built in 1865 and was moved in 1867 to outside the city of Cambridge. Like the Oldfield Church, "the Rock" doubled as both a place of worship and a school. The Rock church, along with its affiliated school, known as Stanley Institute, is listed on the National Register of Historic Places.[56]

Church Creek is home to the oldest continuously run church in the United States, built by British colonists circa 1675. A Protestant Episcopal church originally known simply as Dorchester Parish, it sits a mere three miles west of Vaughn Chapel and has white congregants. It is today referred to as "Old Trinity" and operates under the auspices of the Episcopal Diocese of Easton, in communion with the archbishop of Canterbury. Maryland and Dorchester County Archives have a wealth of history on the church. Its social media presence depicts its current racially homogeneous status, favoring people with European ethnicities and devoid of its neighboring population of Black residents.

In stark contrast with Trinity Church, little has been done to preserve the history of free and prosperous communities connected to Vaughn Chapel, the Rock Church, or Malone's Church.[57] Black churches were one of the few approved places where Black people could commune privately. The covert planning that allowed Tubman to conduct multiple trips through Dorchester County without ever being captured required assistance from the larger Black community.

Preservation efforts of Malone's Church began in 2024 to honor about 40 free families, where, like Oldfield, many intermarried and later owned land. Common surnames are Cornish, Keene, Opher, Henry, Ross, Macer, Stanley, and Travers – which are similar to Oldfield. Interred at Malone's Cemetery are Civil War veterans and members of Harriet Tubman's family.[58]

Across the Chesapeake Bridge, Baltimore's Rev. Calvin Keene is scheduled to retire in 2025 as pastor of Memorial Baptist Church. He is also the leader of a broad-based interfaith and multiracial community power organization. His late mother Rosie (née Stewart) was an officer with the same organization, Baltimoreans United In Leadership Development (BUILD). And as folks say, "he gets it honestly." The pastor is a direct descendant of the distinguished Rev. Charles and Lucinda Keene.

The Afro often preserves genealogical finds that both personalize the struggles of the great migration and help reunify extended family branches that broke from the root. How Judge Josiah Henry Jr. (1893-1980) went from hawking ice cream in Cambridge as a teenager in 1913 to becoming a successful lawyer and then a magistrate at Baltimore City Traffic Court is a true-life rags-to-riches story detailed by The Afro. Another Afro article shows George R. Keene (1893-1962), the only son of Beverly school's celebrated teacher John H. Keene, as a lay church leader whoestablished early childhood education program in 1946. DNA matches confirm the WWI Navy fireman and engineman from Baltimore as this writer's third cousin, three times removed.

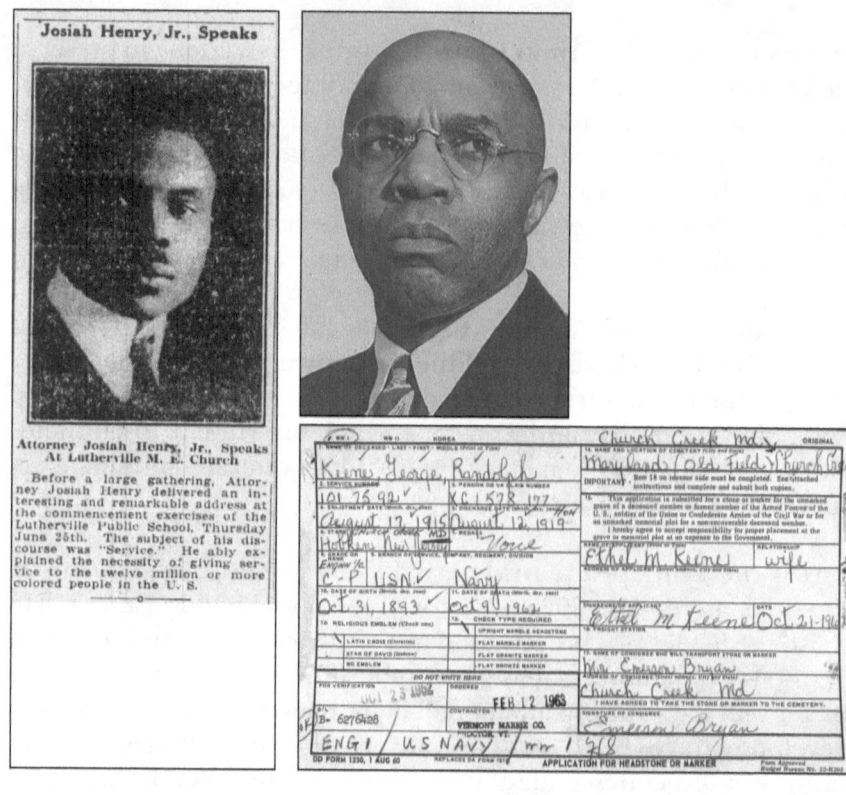

L to R Josiah Henry Jr. Commencement speaker Lutherville Public High School. July 4, 1925. George R. Keene. Church lay leader. US Navy Veteran of WWI. May 18, 1946. Both photos courtesy of Afro American Newspapers Archives/Afro Charities. Applications for headstones for U.S. Military Veterans. National Archives at Washington, D.C. 1925-1941. Courtesy of Ancestry.com. Lehi, UT.

Chapter 5

Oldfield Cemetery

Ceremonial burials at Oldfield Cemetery provide more than comfort to those in mourning; they connect the past with the present. A walk through the field of stone markers is a reminder of a time when the future was uncertain. While the living was never easy under oppressive systems, the closeness of family was restorative. As was their intent, humble ancestors took many stories to the grave with them.

Oldfield Cemetery—the final resting place of more than fifty Civil War U.S. Colored troops (USCT) veterans—is a solemn reminder that many of those Black men who fought for the Union experienced only a modicum of the freedom promised to them by a country that never intended to provide more. This distinction alone should make this cemetery worthy of a historical marker—but there is none.

Oldfield Cemetery is on the north side of Old Field Road, east of the intersection with Golden Hill Road (Maryland 335) and adjacent to the church. The community-led school was directly across the road on the south side. While the Visitor Center at the Harriet Tubman UGRR Museum in Church Creek recommends a self-guided driving tour to view Oldfield's church and cemetery (and the site of the former school), travelers are discouraged from stopping along Oldfield Road because of swampy conditions. With a little caution, visitors would see that USCT veterans are joined by veterans of all of the nation's subsequent wars and conflicts as the unheralded fight for liberation continued on the Eastern Shore.

The property deed that transferred land to cemetery trustees, shows Rev. William D. Vaughn Sr. "and others" paid seventy-five dollars to the Linthicum family for the land on what is now Oldfield Road "to be used soley [*sic*] for a burying ground or cemetery for the burial of colored persons of Church Creek District [...] the remaining portion of said land to be used for camp meetings and picnics [...] for the best interest and enjoyment of the colored people of said district."[59]

Today, descendants own significant tracts of land on Oldfield and Egypt Roads. The community association owns the land where the church and cemetery are located. Included in every Oldfield reunion brochure is a credit to John Fisher (c. 1825-1918), a local preacher and USCT veteran who, along with his wife Celia "Jane" (née Cornish), gifted the land on which a new Vaughn Chapel church was built.[60]

The Fishers are buried at Oldfield along with their daughter Rosetta Dixon (c. 1850-99), and an adopted daughter Jessie Keene (1890-1961), and their close relatives. Pioneers in their own right, Celia Jane Fisher and her granddaughter Martha Dixon may not have thought themselves to be visionaries, but their enduring efforts ensured their loved ones would be buried with dignity.

For over 130 years, the responsibility for maintenance, upkeep, and recordkeeping for Oldfield's cemetery has fallen to volunteers. Descendants convene every spring for the annual cleanup. Flooding is a problem for the cemetery, just as it was 150 years ago for the Black children who traversed swampy land to attend the neighboring school.

Oldfield is not alone. Many historic landmarks along the 125-mile scenic route known as the Harriet Tubman UGRR Byway are in danger of being washed away. Despite their dedication, volunteers have been fighting a losing battle against the effects of climate change, which threatens both this cemetery and nearby Harrisville's Malone Cemetery, where known members of Harriet Tubman's family are buried – but for how long?

Using state-awarded grant money, preservationists of Malone's Church brought in gravel and dirt to build up low levels. Organized as the Harrisville Malone Cemetery Maintenance Fund, its non-profit is working to stabilize the structure and turn the church into an interpretive center. Oldfield continues to rely on volunteers who are descendants of the community to battle the effects of climate change.[61]

Church Creek, considered part of the greater Cambridge area, is surrounded by the federal government's Blackwater National Wildlife Refuge (BNWR), established in 1933. Of its 57,000 acres, over twenty thousand acres are open to public recreation on parcels of land, some of which were owned by free and previously enslaved people of Oldfield.[62]

"Since 1933, when Blackwater became part of the National Wildlife Refuge System, sea level rise has turned 5,000 acres of tidal marsh, with its well-defined river channels, creeks, and ponds, into open water," wrote Rosanne Skirble in October 2021.[63]

Military Veterans and Family Plots

Many grave markers are adorned by crosses, signaling veterans' allegiance to this nation's promise of inclusion, all while serving in racially segregated military units. Comforted by their Christian beliefs, survivors carried on the faith that they would reconnect with their mother, husband, son, and daughter in the next life. Although records are incomplete, USCT veterans are by far the largest represented veteran group at Oldfield, with over fifty names buried at the site. See Chart 2 in the Appendix for a partial list of burials.[64]

Oldfield is largely represented in two USCT regiments that were organized in Baltimore, the 4th and 39[th,] as well as those who traveled nearly directly across the Chesapeake Bay to Southern Maryland's Camp Stanton.[65]

USCT. Regiment 4, Company E. circa 1863. Library of Congress.

The first Regiment of Black soldiers organized to fight for the Union was in the northern state of Massachusetts in early 1863. That summer, Harriet Tubman provided aid and comfort to soldiers from the Black 54th Regiment at Folly Beach, S.C. Perhaps Tubman's most famous military feat was her leadership during the Combahee Ferry Raid in South Carolina, which freed over 700 enslaved Black people. Tubman later took a role in recruiting soldiers. Black units began organizing in the South, with the border state of Maryland taking the lead.

Given that the 54th Regiment was the first organized, and because of Denzel Washington's portrayal in the movie *Glory*, which won an NAACP Image Award, it is arguably most widely known. However, the South's 4th Regiment from Baltimore is perhaps the most recognized because its iconic photograph is widely used to represent the USCT in its entirety.

Those who survived were among the last to return home, mustered out May 4, 1866, thirteen months after General Robert E. Lee surrendered at Appomattox Court House in Virginia. The Army's 39th regiment maintained its all-Black racially segregated status when it was reorganized in future military campaigns. When engaged in the "Indian Wars" of the 1870s, the Black regiments became known as "Buffalo Soldiers," given their prowess and ability to navigate terrains.[66]

Without adequate and consistent recordkeeping of burials sites, a visual of headstones reveals veterans of other wars are also interred at Oldfield Cemetery: WWI: Thomas E. Jackson, George R. Keene, William J. Manokey, Thomas J. Vaughn, George A. Woolford; WWII: Orville Perry, Thomas James, James A. Vaughn, Daniel Weeks; Vietnam: Charles M. King:; Theodore W. Hill; Charles King.[67]

The first recorded burials at Oldfield Cemetery are of members of the Hughes family, one of the oldest families among Dorchester County's free Black population. The family patriarch, Littleton Hughes (c 1800-1876), left a paper trail of communications with the U.S. War Department that illuminates the sacrifices families made in service to the country. He and his wife, Hester (née Atkinson), are listed in the 1840 census as free inhabitants of Dorchester County with three sons and two daughters. In the 1850 census, they are listed by name along with their 10 children.[68]

In one egregious case of ethical misconduct, William Hughes (1845-64), who enlisted in August 1863 at age 19, never returned from the war. Family patriarch Rev. Littleton Hughes fought for a decade to obtain details of his son's fate. Years later, he finally learned that his son had died in a hospital just after the war, but a white local businessman named Daniel T. Orem (1831-97) had already filed for and received death benefits for the young man. Williams' remains were never returned.

Proof that Orem's actions regarding William were not clerical oversights but a character flaw is revealed once he secured bounty proceeds that were due to Littleton's older son, Alexander (1844-89), and his widow, Hester (née Johnson). Hester's complaint stated that Orem fraudulently withheld bounty proceeds once Alexander Hughes died and left behind minor children. Depositions were filed by Alexander's brother-in-law, Rufus Jarmon, as well as the elder William D. Vaughn (father of the man for whom Vaughn Chapel is named), who signed an affidavit in 1893 attesting to the couple's marriage. See Letters 1, 2, and 3 in the Appendix for pension awards and complaints.

The Hughes family plot at Oldfield Cemetery includes Littleton's sons Alexander, Henry Ebenezer "Eben" (d. 1897), and Francis/Frank (d. 1890), and his daughter Louisa (d. 1898). Another daughter, Sarah (d. September 1915), is thought to be buried there as well. Sarah and her husband, Rufus Jarmon, are the ancestors of William Jarmon, a past OFCCCIA president.

Prominent Family Plots

Most of the cemetery's earliest burials came from Black families that had been free prior to the war. Some of the most notable free people include: William Bailey, Reverends John S. and Sarah Cromwell, Elizabeth Ennals, William "Bill" and Ellen Kiah, Alexander and Louisa (née Keene) Plater, Susan Ross, James Macer, Benjamin Vaughn, and John H. Keene.

While the Clash and Marine families were integral to the growth of Oldfield, there does not appear to be a family plot for either.[69] Other prominent family surnames, such as Bailey, Camper, and Cornish, have small plots in Oldfield. On the other hand, there are families with relatively larger representation in the cemetery, including the surnames of Chester, Ennals, Henry, Keene, Kiah, Plater, Macer, Manokey, Ross, Vaughn, and Woolford.

The genealogy that connects Oldfield to Harriet (Ross) Tubman is explored in Chapter Seven. Buried at Oldfield include: Susan Ross (1869-1949), Alexander (1880-1955), Birstal Ross (1895-1963), Edward C. Ross (1889-1959), John W. Ross (1898-1952), Winfield H. Ross (1893-1984), and his wife Mary (1900-94).

John H. Keene, born in Madison, moved to Oldfield in 1887 and taught at Beverly for 13 years. He instructed over a dozen students who successfully passed the state Board of Education exam for teachers.

A skilled wrestler, carpenter, and reluctant farmer, Keene built a thirty-two-foot sailboat that was the fastest at the time.

The Plater family was helmed by its matriarch, Rachel (née Farrow) Plater (c 1820-1929), who lived to be over 100 years old and is buried in nearby Cambridge.[70] She and her husband George Plater's known children include son Alexander (1851-1912) and daughter Carmena Thompson (c. 1855- 1914).

Alexander and his wife, Louisa (née Keene) (1848-1916), had 11 children, and all of them have descendants with DNA in national databases. Affectionately known as "Mother Plater," the centenarian was a grandmother to dozens and a mother figure to the entire community and is discussed in greater detail in the genealogy chapter.

The Plater family plot at Oldfield includes Alexander and Louisa and their son Palestine Plater (1875-1960), his wife Martha (née Dixon) (1878-1956), and stepson William "David" Vaughn (1901-80). The longest survivor of the couple's eight children raised on their Egypt Road farm was Mildred (née Plater) Hughes (1917-2016). A frequent attendee of the annual Memorial Day and heritage weekends, Mildred was buried in Oldfield Cemetery with her husband, Phillip Lee Hughes, a US Army WWII veteran.

East Baltimore's own Ethel (née Keene) Dean, mentioned previously as pivotal in the establishment of the Baltimore chapter of Oldfield's community association, is buried with her husband at Oldfield Cemetery. They are the direct ancestors of Monica R. J. Bland, the impetus and organizer of the 130th commemoration of Vaughn Chapel Church in 2024.

Dangerous Waters

Despite the treacherous roads and sinking headstones at Oldfield due to grading and lapses in sediment control, each Memorial Day, people gather to recognize the labor and sacrifices of those who answered the call to defend the country.

The centerpiece of the 125-mile Harriet Tubman Byway self-guided tour from Maryland to Philadelphia is a visitor center opened in 2017. While built to withstand flooding, not a decade later, the flat lands are losing ground to rising sea levels, unable to be significantly stymied by the marshes and tidal wetlands.

Church Creek, the closest legal entity to Oldfield/Beverly, is named on the tour as one of the places where free Black sailors known as "Black Jacks" passed along secret communications from their maritime network as part of the UGRR. Water was not a hindrance to those seeking to escape bondage; it actually was an asset for those travelling the most surreptitious routes possible.

Maritime trades such as caulkers, sail makers, and blacksmiths were common for free Black people who brought news, ideas, and the all-essential means to escape slavery throughout nearby coastal towns.

The same navigational and tracking skills that were passed along the UGRR for generations were employed by Buffalo soldiers who impressed Native Americans. Regrettably, the natural landmarks Tubman used as navigational tools are in danger. "[…] these marshes are being lost to the rising ocean at an alarming rate and could be underwater by 2050," from the Union of Concerned Scientists 2014 report "National Landmarks at Risk."[71]

In 2025, the Dorchester County council passed a bill to preserve area cemeteries by establishing a burial sites preservation board. The board's duties are to take inventory of all known sites and establish guidelines for supervision, maintenance, repair, and reconstruction in conjunction with the Dorchester County Historical Society and Maryland Historical Trust.

Stemming the tides has been a literal and figurative endeavor for people whose labor earned them a final resting place on land owned that has been continuously owned by members of their community.

Old Field Road street sign 2019. Photo by Keesha Ha.

Chapter 6

Dorchester's First School for Black Students

The story of Dorchester County's first school for Black students often begins with the arrival of a young white woman from Massachusetts to the Blackwater region of Maryland's Eastern Shore in fall 1865. The often-overlooked prologue is that Oldfield residents schooled themselves, generations before her arrival, when it was a punishable crime to do so.

Mary S. Osbourne (1839-73) brought resources to an otherwise under supported school within the Oldfield Church that had been operating since at least 1830 (prior to Nat Turner's 1831 rebellion). With the labor and materials donated by Oldfield residents themselves once a formal structure was in place, the community-owned school was named for the Beverly chapter of the New England Freedmen's Aid Society, which sponsored Osbourne's travel and service. Both Osbourne and her younger sister, Elmira Isabel Osbourne (1843-1931), were teachers in Dorchester County as part of the Freedmen's Bureau's education program.

Gratitude is certainly owed to Osbourne, who was steadfast in her mission to establish the first formal school for Black students after the Civil War, even when threatened, cursed, and ostracized by members of the larger white community. Armed with Bible scriptures to support their white supremacist beliefs, Osbourne did not reconcile that her fellow worshippers at the racially segregated Methodist church were the same people who upheld the systems determined to dehumanize Black people and deny them a proper education.[72]

Oldfield School's true origin story of free and literate Black people can be traced to when Harriet Tubman's parents themselves were still children, yet it has been largely left out of history books. Literate free Black people lived in Maryland as early as the 18th century, notes a local scholar, Dr. Kay Najiyyah McElvey. Those with African ancestry in Dorchester County fought valiantly in the Revolutionary War as well, McElvey asserts in her 1990 dissertation.[73]

In October 1865, Osbourne wrote to the Baltimore Association for the Moral and Educational Improvement of the Colored People about her first month at the school that was organized and financially supported by the Oldfield community. The historical marker for Stanley Institute, founded in 1867 depicts it as the only existing community-owned school in the county, but it was not the first.[74]

Once the county instituted its public school system, Beverly became known as Colored School No. 1. It was torn down sometime around the 1950s, with little documentation that recognized its significance.

Colored School No. 2, where Mary's sister Isabel Osbourne is believed to have been a teacher, was intact as late as 2002 when preservation efforts began. Once racial school integration was enacted, the Black-owned and operated school was taken over by the state board of education before Church Creek's municipal commissioners sold it to the Vickers family. It has since been demolished.[75]

In its 2002 report and evaluation, the Maryland Historical Trust found that "[Colored School No. 2] is an important local vestige of Reconstruction-era rural education facilities… [and] an excellent example of an unaltered rural nineteenth-century schoolhouse. Occupying the same lot within the borough since its construction, the building is an important component of the Church Creek streetscape."[76]

The report dates the school was constructed between1872-1877 in response to the state's first laws that established schools for Black students post-emancipation. The Trust deemed it "significant" under National Register criteria as the only remaining education facility in Church Creek occupying the same lot since construction as a symbol of "community education." It also noted that the local municipality was planning to sell it to a private buyer.[77]

"Colored School" No. 2 in Church Creek. (September 2002). Courtesy of Maryland Historical Trust.

When it comes to failures to archive and recognize the historical significance of its Black residents, as shown with the 2006 land deed transfer to the Vickers family, Dorchester County's institutions have demonstrated a recent and distant history of subverting Black education.

In 1886, Osbourne captured the sentiment of a representative of the larger community in a published letter that details the demeanor and attitudes of Mrs. Hoddinott, the proprietor of the house where Osbourne stayed while in Oldfield.

"Mrs. H," as Osbourne referred to her, was described as having eyes that were once blue "but now have faded to a nameless hue," and she subjected the young teacher to a barrage of disparaging comments about local Blacks. Osbourne wrote about the conversations in a way that captured the dialect of "Mrs. H's" style of speaking:

> "I won't have my chillren put on 'quality wid niggers; niggers ain't nothin' no ways'…this lecture lasted for nearly two hours; much of the language used was too low to be written.[78]

Speaking of Daniel T. Orem's character, Mary Osbourne credited him for serving as a buffer against the vitriol spewed by Dorchester's white population when she arrived. But Orem himself was no friend of the Black population. When Black people in the county experienced some measure of freedom, it was by forcibly removing the chains themselves.

Uneducated by Design: Systemic Racism

As a colony and then as a young state, Maryland failed in its attempt to fund a public education system, even with revenue streams from taxing fur exports, Irish Catholic indentured servants, and the extremely lucrative involuntary and life-long bondage of people transported from Africa.

An influx of federal subsidies in 1825 led to the appointment of county school commissioners, but even then, standards were not implemented across the state. Without state support, ethnic and religious groups were responsible for administering a plethora of community-owned schools that lacked vigorous academic standards.

Maryland's status as a border state and Baltimore's growth as a port city with a large concentration of free Black people was a unique condition for educational opportunities. Founded in 1828 in connection with the Oblate Sisters of Providence convent, St. Francis Academy for girls was a beacon for those seeking to educate Black children across the South and in the Caribbean. It consistently is ranked high among the private schools in Baltimore.

However, after Nat Turner led a revolt against slavery in Virginia in 1831, the political tides turned. It became dangerous (or illegal, depending on the state) for free or enslaved Black people to learn how to read or write. The education of Black children began to be seen by white people as a threat. The job of Paddyrollers, who once solely hunted fugitives from slavery, extended to confronting those who aided people of African ancestry to read and write.

By 1840, Maryland had no intention of educating its Black population, refusing to implement any system towards that end, leaving communities largely on their own. Black church leaders often assumed educational duties. In Baltimore, ethnic and religious groups operated their own schools. It was not until 1865, the end of the Civil War, that Maryland passed a public education law that included the education of Black students (if under state control). Maryland did not join the Confederacy, even though Baltimore's council voted in favor of seceding and was largely considered an ally of Virginia.[79]

An emotional appeal made in 1870 by Maryland's first state school superintendent to include Black students in the education system depicts more progressive values than Osbourne could have summoned for herself. Even in advocating racially segregated schools, Rev. Dr. Libertus Van Bokkelen made an impassioned plea:

> These people, for many years, have been to us faithful servants; they have tilled our fields and worked in our dwellings, performing acceptably all those duties which increase the convenience and comforts of social life. They have been our hewers of wood and drawers of water. Generation after generation has followed our

bidding and helped to earn for us what we possess . . . Now that they are free and provide for themselves—our duty is to educate them.[80]

Farther north, in the larger city of Cambridge, two schools that opened after Beverly have wider notoriety, largely because of organized community involvement and grant funding. Cambridge teacher David "Nicky" Henry includes remembrances of both of these Cambridge schools in his 2003 book *Up Pine Street*. The first, Jenifer Institute ("Colored" School No.1), is associated with the popular Waugh Chapel Church. Another, the Stanley Institute (or "Rock School," "Colored School" No.3), was relocated from Church Creek in 1867, where it became a school and meetinghouse. Located at 2439 Rock Drive in Cambridge, Stanley Institute was listed on the National Register of Historic Places in 1975, according to the state's architectural file for historical preservation.[81]

Left: Mary S. (née Osbourne) Sayer (Circa 1873). Isabell (née Osbourne) Yorty and daughter Elsia May (1900). Courtesy of the Yorty family.

The Freedmen's Bureau funded Osbourne's salary and provided materials until 1872, when the bureau was dismantled. After that time, Oldfield students paid tuition so that the community-owned school could be maintained. In describing the Beverly as the "oldest Dorchester County school for black children," A. M. Foley and Gloria Johnson-Mansfield wrote in 2002:

"Established before the close of the Civil War, [Beverly School] was, of necessity, staffed initially by whites, two sisters [Mary and Isabel Osbourne] who came to Old Field from Massachusetts."[82]

Veterans' Benefits: A Community Chest

Daniel T. Orem (1831-97) and his wife Dorothy (née Busick), for the nominal fee of five dollars, sold land to Oldfield residents as trustees upon which they built the Beverly School. The formidable Rev. Charles Keene (born free and not a veteran) and his wife Lucinda are listed as trustees along with ten other men from Oldfield. Two were USCT veterans from the 4th Regiment: Cpl. William J. Stiles (Co. D) and John Fisher (Co. E).[83]

It is unclear whether another trustee, Jeremiah Marine, is the USCT veteran Reg 4 Co E whose widow pension was received by Orem, who died in 1866, or a person with the same name who was a local farmer who died c1885.

Orem declared the small lot of land was "for the purpose of erecting or allowing to be erected thereon a School House for the use, benefit and education of the Colored People of the State of Maryland in Dorchester County, forever."[84]

Orem's motives for aiding in the establishment of Beverly school cannot be accurately discerned, but his actions are questionable. Orem's filings for bankruptcy are a matter of public record. A deep dive into his financial activity reveals that he routinely swindled veterans' benefits from Black families for his own personal financial gain. Portions of his wealth (that he used to purchase Oldfield land that he later sold) were obtained from fraudulent claims he made to the Freedmen's Bureau.

As calls to war, disease, physical labor, and lack of health care hastened the lives of many men, the widows of Oldfield were fierce matriarchs who eventually stood toe to toe with Orem. Two women, both widows of Civil War veterans, were essential in the establishment of Oldfield: Rosetta (James) Dixon and Hester (John) Montgomery. They each purchased land from local merchant Daniel T. Orem and his wife shortly after the end of the war. The land transactions appear to be restitution for Orem's fraudulently pocketing their widow's pension payments. See Letter 1 in the Appendix for Littleton Hughes' complaint.

Orem figures prominently as both a hindrance and a help to Oldfield residents during Reconstruction, as he was the local postmaster and used his gravitas as a former delegate to Abraham Lincoln to expedite pension applications. Over a dozen complaints that Orem fraudulently claimed pension and bounty payments made to the Freedmen's Bureau include:

- In November 1868, Hester Montgomery reported that Orem fraudulently collected her widow's pension payments totaling $611.
- In January 1869, Jeremiah Marine's widow (Adella) complained that she received only $90 from her husband's $300 benefit through Daniel T. Orem.
- In March 1869, Orem sold land to Hester Montgomery for $300.
- In October 1871, Rev. Littleton (spelled Lyttleton in the records) Hughes reported to the bureau that it had been nine years since Orem had collected the pension for his deceased son William and kept the proceeds. The reverend, a patriarch with ten children, committed suicide five years after filing the complaint. Two of Littleton's sons, Alexander (also a USCT veteran) and Henry Ebenezer "Eben," were the first two people interred at Oldfield's cemetery.

The men and women of Oldfield who watched their family, friends, and neighbors get bought and sold purchased the land upon which they stood once they were free. As both patrons and benefactors, they directed the use of their own labor and materials and built the community's institutions. When self-determination was at hand, they allowed leaders to emerge to guide the path forward.

In Mary Osbourne's Own Words

Newspapers are useful primary sources for the historical context of the time period and regional customs. Obituaries, tributes, criminal trials, court proceedings, and land records are stalwarts for researchers. If one is lucky enough, newspapers sometimes yield a photograph or even a letter to the editor that captures the words, inflections, and attitudes of its writer.

In a series of articles Osbourne published in the Methodist periodical *Zion's Herald* under the title "Among the Freedmen," she provided a unique firsthand account of a time and a community otherwise absent from the annals of history.

Osbourne's lack of understanding of the impact of colonialism was on full display in the Methodist periodical: "they [Black students] copy the styles of their white neighbors with a dexterity that would do honor to the Chinese," she wrote in 1866. Cornrows ("caterpillar-like arrangements") in children's hair, while neatly coiffed, were not viewed as aesthetically pleasing. "As I shall insist upon the daily use of the comb among my pupils."[85]

In the series' first article, published in 1865, Osbourne detailed her arrival in the southern city of Baltimore before taking a ship to Cambridge on Maryland's Eastern Shore. She mentioned the infamous stench of Baltimore's decrepit sewers as well as the spectacular abundance and variety at the city's famed Lexington Market. A city equally famous for having the nation's largest and most prosperous population of free Blacks before the war, Osbourne was surprised to find that "colored schools were in "excellent order," with attendance at one thousand students, operating both day and night.[86]

One particular observation that Osbourne recounted in her January 17, 1866, article is of immense interest to this writer, being a direct descendant of Charles and Lucinda (Henry) Keene. Keene, the first trustee listed on the land deed for the school, was father of twelve and, eventually, grandfather of about forty-one. His certificate of freedom entry describes him as chestnut color. It states that he was born free circa 1820 to a manumitted mother, Ann, which is explored more in chapter 6. One of the few public services designed to aid the history of Black Marylanders in the state archives is a searchable database of certificates of freedom and manumission records.

Osbourne wrote: "Rev. Charles Keene (colored) has been in to see me. He is one of the most influential men among the colored people here. He told me he had 'twelve heads of children to send to school.' He is *very* black [emphasis added] but has a sensible face, which made me feel at once that I was conversing with a man."[87]

In various reports, Osbourne noted that the students who gathered at the Oldfield Church school ranged in age from six to thirty-five. Many knew only the alphabet, but she noted that the Hughes children were accomplished readers. With the encouragement of Osbourne, members of the Hughes, Clash, and Vaughn families relocated to Rhode Island.[88]

As a Yankee visitor to Maryland's Eastern Shore, Osbourne imposed her northern white privilege not only on the students but on her white host family as well. She described her "boarding house mistress" as a "pale, then, bony woman" with eyes "That were once blue but now have faded to a nameless hue" with teeth "black, broken and decayed protruded over her under lip." In 1866, Osbourne lamented the conditions:

> How am I to endure this all winter? I will not anticipate; if [Mrs. Hoddinott] does not direct the sharp-shooting of her tongue at me, perhaps I can bear it. A 'colored

teacher' cannot afford to be fastidious about board-ing-places, for I am told there are not more than three families in the place who would entertain me at their tables on any account[...][89]

Telling Our Own Stories

Generations believe that Daniel T. Orem was Dorchester County's equivalent to John Brown. Adding insult to injury, through the lens of Black lives being inconsequential, Church Creek municipal leaders gave away land and an intact and invaluable 19th-century school structure. The onus is on descendants of all Black communities to amplify the lives of those dismissed and disenfranchised and prevent the erasure of a part of the annals of U.S. history.

While Beverly, as the first Black school in the county, has been largely forgotten by history, the ancillary role of a singular white man has been overemphasized. Largely known during his time for operating a store and being postmaster, the Dorchester County native has been celebrated posthumously as an abolitionist.

In a common revisionist history tactic, the *Salisbury Times* in 1959 reported that Orem was an "ardent abolitionist" when "Many of his neighbors were not." The article's focus was on his motive behind building his house in Church Creek as a replica of Lincoln's estate in Springfield, IL. Underlining the importance of oral history, instead of being known as the "Lincoln House," locals often refer to the structure as the "Bounty House." [90]

A guest speaker during Oldfield's fall 2005 Heritage Weekend celebra-tion, educator, activist, and historian Dr. Kay Najiyyah McElvey retired after thirty years of teaching in the county's middle school and founded the African American Culture Society while serving on a multitude of boards until her death in 2017. Her research substantiated oral accounts that in the early 1800s, some of Oldfield's residents could both read and write.[91]

McElvey, the daughter of Walter and Mary Johnson, graduated as the valedictorian from Dorchester's high school for Black people (Mace's Lane) in 1962. The lack of Black history resources within the Black community inspired Dr. Kay Najiyyah McElvery's dissertation, which became a 1991 book: *Early Black Dorchester 1776-1870: A history of the struggle of African-Americans in Dorchester County, Maryland, to be free to make their own choices*. She wrote it with the hope that young people derive connectedness and belonging through learning about their history and, as a result, can better choose their destiny, which is similar to the desires of this writer.[92]

Beverly School's Legacy

With the foresight and dedication of the OFCCCIA, established in 1954, Beverly School escaped erasure from the cultural and historical annals. Mary Rachel (Henry) Woolford (1904–2005), who would later serve as association president, attended Beverly School from first through seventh grade.

Woolford's granddaughter, Calmetta Woolford Brinkley, spoke fondly of her grandmother:

> After our mother passed, we were raised by this faithful and loving lady for a year. Precious memories linger in my soul—watching her work magic in the kitchen, canning, baking, and cooking delicious food[...] She raised her ten biological children and grandchildren in times of need. She was always available to assist anyone. She was the Proverbs 31 virtuous woman in every way.[93]

Brinkley spoke, too, of Woolford's love of service: "She loved serving and supporting Vaughn Chapel, its cemetery, and Ross Hall. She loved sharing the history of the Oldfield community. She loved the Lord and her family. At 101 years of age, she encouraged all who would listen to her to 'live a good life.' "[94]

The women of Oldfield trained as teachers, worked as farmers, and organized as activists. Beverly graduate Hattie Waters Hargis (1879–1962) was a trustee of Bennett College in Greensboro, North Carolina, as well as president of Women's Home Missionary Society. In 1927, she fought and won against racial discrimination with the Methodist Episcopal Church in Philadelphia and ended racially segregated eating during church events.[95]

A student of John H. Keene, Martha (Dixon) Vaughn Plater (1878–1956), who was admitted to the State Board of Education, boasts a legacy of educators and leaders. Her great-granddaughter, Dr. Bronte Burleigh-Jones, is an accomplished higher education finance officer, currently at American University in Washington, DC.

Despite recollections that the one-room schoolhouse was directly across the road from the church, the date of its actual demise is unknown, widely believed to have been in the late 1950s. Nonetheless, Beverly School's impact has not been forgotten. The families who invested their energy and materials to build it have paid dividends beyond measure.

The courage of two religious sisters from Massachusetts who committed to their beliefs despite the vitriol espoused by Methodist parishioners in Church Creek is heroic by any standard and any time period.

Certificate of Incorporation   #   Be it remembered and it

    of   " Paid "   # is hereby certified that

Beverly United Stock Club.   # the following Certificate

####################### of Incorporation was received

and recorded on the 2nd day of February, 1921.

    Know all men by these Presents, That we, Thomas Ross,

Aurender J. Vaughn, Charles E. Keene, Benjamin Vaughn and

Frederick Kane, all of Dorchester County, State of Maryland,

being citizens of the United States, and a majority of us

citizens of the State of Maryland, do hereby certify that

we do, under and by virtue of the GENERAL LAWS of this

State authorizing the formation of corporations, hereby form

a corporation under the name of THE BEVERLY UNITED STOCK

CLUB of Dorchester County, Maryland.

    We do further certify that the said corporation so formed

is a corporation for the purpose of buying personal property

lands, and making loans, that the terms of existence of the

Beverly United Stock Club's Charter

Chapter 7

Beverly United Stock Club

Inspired by Tulsa's thriving Black Wall Street following Reconstruction, a few courageous men of Oldfield organized the Beverly United Stock Club on Maryland's Eastern Shore. Beginning about 1918, their investments not only expanded the antebellum-era settlement of Oldfield but also led to its rebranding as a vibrant village under the new name of "Beverly."

Somehow avoiding the racial violence and burned businesses that wrecked Tulsa, OK, the club strengthened the communal roots of the forgotten people who were once essential to the UGRR. Over the course of the next forty years, farmers, craftsmen, and laborers made a way out of no way by shoring up the swampy land that their ancestors had trodden for two hundred years.

Club members purchased hundreds of acres of land in the county, which provided an economic foundation that paved the way for today's scholars and achievers. Tax rolls from the early 1900s show residents on both Old Field and Egypt Roads in Church Creek as property owners on the very soil that Tubman once trod as she guided family, friends, and neighbors to freedom from being bought and sold as property.

Spared the fate of Tulsa's 1921 massacre of its Black citizens, the educated business people of Oldfield won multiple battles against the county and the state to accumulate land for Beverly expansion. But they eventually lost the war against the United States Fish and Wildlife Service with the continued expansion of the Blackwater National Wildlife Refuge.

Against the backdrop of violence, the entrepreneurial spirit transformed the swampy village of Oldfield into a cozy farming community known as Beverly. Lynchings were prevalent in the adjacent counties of Wicomico and Somerset over the course of the four decades of investment activity by club members. A similar historic Black Florida community, Rosewood, was burned and its residents massacred by a mob of white men in 1923.

In 1912, white mobs drove out Black residents of Oscarville, GA, by gunpoint, and the US Army Corps of Engineers flooded the once vibrant economic center for Blacks in the 1950s. Black towns across the South, such as Kowaliga, AL, and Little Egypt, NC, were intentionally submerged using eminent domain to create recreational lakes and reservoirs.[96]

Origins and Organization

On September 11, 1920, brothers Benjamin and Arender J. "A. J." Vaughn and brothers Charles and Frederick Keene joined Thomas Ross as charter members of Beverly United Stock Club. The certificate of incorporation was recorded on February 2, 1921. The organization thrived for more than four decades under multiple leaders.

The five named directors managed the corporation for the first year, with new leadership advancing the mission over the corporation's lifespan. The certificate of incorporation filed with the State of Maryland shows that the five men pooled $1,500 ($25,000 in today's valuation), which represented "fifteen shares of the par value of one hundred dollars each."[97]

The charter members embraced Beverly as the preferred name of their hometown over "Oldfield." Perhaps the rebranding was necessary to forge a financially secure future that involved navigating unfamiliar legal and economic systems designed to keep them oppressed.

The surnames of the stock club members reveal many connections to the first families of Oldfield: Bishop, Bowley, Bryan, Cummings, Dixon, Fisher, Henry, Hughes, Kane, Keene, Linthicum, Macer, Manokey, Montgomery, Plater, Ross, Vaughn, Williams, Wilson, and Woolford.

Two charter members, the Keene brothers, are the grandsons of Beverly school administrator Rev. Charles and his wife, Lucinda (Henry) Keene (Kane and Keen are spelling variations). The pair were no strangers to financial dealings. In 1866, their grandfather, Rev. Keene, purchased seventy-three acres of Oldfield land that would later become essential to Oldfield's growth as part of a bounty homesteading program for his military service.[98]

Two other charter members, the Vaughn brothers, are nephews of Oldfield founder William D. Vaughn Sr. Their sister, Ida Vaughn, married fellow charter member Thomas Ross, making him their brother-in-law. The only known woman club member, Emma (Nicols) Henry Vaughn, was the widow of Simeon Henry and later A.J. Vaughn.

The Club's initial pooled investment of $1,500 yielded an immeasurable return. What they could not have planned in 1924 was that 100 years later, their efforts ingrained the significance of a small Eastern Shore settlement in the history of Black American culture.

The meetings were both business and social gatherings. The *Baltimore Afro-American Newspaper* covered the club's meeting in its May 2, 1924, edition, along with other issues that related to Oldfield:

> The Beverly United Stalk [sic] Club met at the residence of Mr. Benjamin Vaugh[n] Monday night to arrange for a picnic. Many visitors were present, and after business was over, refreshments were served. Mr. Arender Vaughn, president; Mr. Charley Keene,

secretary[...] the Building committee met at the Church in Beverly to make preparations to begin to rebuild in May. T. H. Ross, chairman, Charles Keene, secretary, Rev. L.H. Martin, pastor.[99]

Oldfield and Harriet Tubman

Harriet Tubman's unique navigation skills are justly credited for the estimated thirteen successful trips to and from Maryland, with a portion likely either through or near Oldfield. Acclaimed for never having lost a "passenger" across rugged terrain and rough waterways, Tubman led many family members, friends, and neighbors out of the bondage of slavery in Dorchester County. However, the link between the family of Harriet Tubman and the land where free and enslaved Black people built the community of Oldfield has not been recognized until this publishing.

Many have noted that an essential factor in the UGRR's longevity was the unwavering aid of freedmen like Rev. Charles Keene and William Vaughn, who offered safe passage, refuge, supplies, and silence. As station agents at the point of departure, Oldfield residents had a crucial responsibility not to yield to the pressure and threats of enslavers chasing freedom seekers who had fled north.

In about 1855, Tubman led her niece, Kessiah (née Jolley) Bowley, and her family away from their Dorchester County enslavers during slave auction proceedings to points north where slavery was illegal. By way of secret messages, all aspects of the plan were put into motion, Kate Clifford Larson wrote in her biography *Bound for the Promised Land*. Two years later, the couple's son, Harkless Bowley, was born in Canada, home to Tubman and other family members.

> "Harriet and Kessiah's husband, John Bowley, devised a scheme to spirit Kessiah and her two children away [...] the auctioneer started the bidding again, only to discover that Kessiah and the children were nowhere to be found [...] she and the children had been taken

and hidden in a nearby house" according to an account provided by Harkless Bowley.[100]

After the war, the Bowleys (Boley, Bailey, and Bayley are all variations in spelling) returned to Dorchester County and purchased land in Oldfield. The 1870 census shows the couple living in Church Creek with sons Harkless, Josiah, and John R., and daughter Pleasant.

Harkless graduated from high school, married, had a family, and later moved to Washington, DC, where he worked as a civil servant. He visited his relatives in New York and Canada, including Harriet Tubman.

Fittingly, one of the club's first purchases was the land that John Francis Henry bought from Harkness and Rachel J. Bowley in 1924. The land connects the Oldfield community to the niece that Harriet Tubman shepherded from bondage to freedom. This transaction represented one of the club's first purchases.[101]

Club Investments

The corporation's charter stated that it was organized "for the purpose of buying personal property, lands, and making loans," mostly in the small town of Church Creek. For the four decades it was consistently active, the club was successful in making property owners out of local residents who had limited education as farmers, watermen, and laborers. [102]

The club's business model evolved from exchange between friends and neighbors to a practice of capitalizing on undervalued properties put up for tax sale by the county. The club purchased three acres in Cambridge at a price of five dollars in a county tax sale in November 1928. In June 1931, A. J. Vaughn, as president, and Charles E. Keene, as secretary, sold the property to George Spence and his wife for $150—a return on investment of 2,900 percent over two and a half years. This business model, though simple, is one that is still used today.[103]

In addition to lending money for farm expansion to the descendants of Oldfield, the club served as a mortgage lender for about a dozen people, setting up a foundation of generational wealth for their families. In one such instance, Thomas and Ida (née Vaughn) Ross purchased five acres of land from the club for one dollar in March 1947. The deed, signed by Wilbert J. Woolford as president and Robert W. Cummings as secretary, reads in part:

> "In the village of 'Old Field' on the easterly side of the 'Old Field' road, adjoining the lands of Emerson Bryan, and lands known as Artemus Mace [...] in Church Creek election District of Dorchester County, Maryland [...] being the same and identical lot of land described in a deed from Leon H. Jones and Mary C. Jones, his wife, to 'The Beverly United Stock Club' dated the 17th day of July, nineteen hundred and thirty-six[...]"[104]

Prior to the Ross family acquiring the land from the club, Leon H. Jones and his wife, who were white, bought the land in a tax sale for twenty-five dollars after the county seized the property due to unpaid taxes by the widow of Civil War veteran John Wesley Montgomery, Hester (née Manokey). Ultimately, with the second tax sale of this property, the club was able to secure ownership of ancestral land.

The most significant land purchase was of a parcel of over fifteen acres that is now largely synonymous with Oldfield itself. It included the Beverly school property. This parcel was transferred on October 6, 1950, to Winfield H. Ross of Baltimore and his wife for $5. Ross later transferred the property's ownership to the OFCCCIA.

The 1950 deed was signed by Rev. J. Wilbert Woolford as president and Jason Henry as secretary; they are widely believed to be the last officers of the club. Rev. Woolford died in 1983 at age eighty-four. His son Louis Wadell Woolford (1924–2022) was a World War II veteran. The Woolfords gather in regular family reunions.[105]

Beverly Stock Club members meeting. Circa 1955.

L to R Seated: Clarence Vaughn, James Bishop, Harrison Chester, Emma Vaughn, Rev. Lewis Bayneum, and Emerson Bryan. 2nd Row: Rev. William West, Charles Keene, Palestine Plater, Walter Wilson. Back row: Wm "David" Vaughn, Rev. J. Wilbert Woolford, Robert Cummings, A.J. Vaughn, Thomas Ross, Charles Manokey, and Jason Henry. Photo Courtesy of OFCCCIA.

The stock club's charter members stood on the shoulders of those who built Oldfield's first church before emancipation and built the county's first school for its Black population once slavery was abolished. After Reconstruction, the interrelationship between economic independence and educational opportunities was a primary focus in Black families and communities, notes journalist Rodney Brooks. The failure of the nation's banking system designed to aid Black people after the war was attributable to many factors, one of which was the practice of whites siphoning away efforts designed to financially restore Black families.[106]

Bravely claiming their right to self-determination and financial independence, the sons and grandsons of Oldfield's free and enslaved Black residents sought to achieve true emancipation. Dorchester's Black men banded together against rising white nationalism, its adherents determined to maintain racial segregation at the expense of human rights.

Chapter 8

Genealogy and the Secrets of DNA

The popularity of genealogy peaked when the television series *Roots* lifted the lid off Pandora's box. Based on Alex Haley's 1976 book, the all-star cast dramatized the often-ignored generational trauma inflicted by this country's human trafficking enterprise. *Roots* laid bare founders' complicity to families gathered in the comfort of their homes. The show's success also fortified the resolve of elders to hold court over the family bible, funeral programs, and scrapbooks that trace family history.

Pandora's Box was then shattered into a million pieces thanks to the advances of technology that brought to light activities most thought could stay buried. Researchers delved into databases, scanned documents, and scoured the Internet, connecting enslavers with the families they enslaved, aided by DNA results.

In the early 2000s, commercially available DNA tests catapulted a resurgent interest in Black familial history. Gen X and Millennials, eager to discover their ethnic origin percentages by deciphering inherited chromosomes, gave birth to genetic genealogy.[107]

Unboxing DNA results for clicks and clout on social media platforms coincided with the rising popularity of television shows like *Finding Your Roots*, *Who Do You Think You Are*, and *Genealogy Roadshow*.

A community of amateur genealogists sleuthing their origins convenes virtually using cell phones and computers, seeking answers to questions that no one ever thought were possible: Where am I from? Where do I belong? What happened to my people?

Mother Plater

Publicly available records documenting births, deaths, and military service, in addition to the federal decennial census, are essential to genealogy. But the most coveted archival documents are photographs. Rumored to be 110 years old, this book's cover photograph of Oldfield's oldest matriarch, Rachel (née Farrow) Plater, who died in 1929, connects hundreds of her descendants.

She and her husband, George Plater (born about 1830), lived in Church Creek their entire lives and were land owners. Of the half dozen children's names included on census records, only their eldest son, Alexander Plater, has known descendants with publicly available DNA results at the time of this writing. No connections to Mother Rachel via her shared DNA on the Ancestry.com database have yielded potential siblings for Mother Plater or clues about her parents.

It is likely that she is the source of DNA markers attributable to tribes of Native Americans that were passed along to her living descendants. Census records suggest that the couple had two other sons, George Jr. and William Plater, but DNA matching has not corroborated this genetic link.

L to R: Rachel Plater (circa 1925). Headstone for Rachel's son Alexander, and his wife Louisa at Oldfield Cemetery. Photos courtesy of the family. State of Maryland death certificate for 110-year-old Rachel.

Of their eleven children, only George and Rachel's son, Alexander has descendants with DNA on the Ancestry website. He and his wife, Louisa Keene (the daughter of Charles Keene, trustee of Beverly School), are known to have had eight daughters and one son – Palestine Plater. Each of the daughters – Wilhelmina (m. Jason Henry) of Cambridge; Rachel (m. Charles Payne) of Philadelphia and Cape May, NJ; Lillie (m. Greenwood Waters) of Baltimore; Bethina (m. Robert Cummings) of Cambridge; AlexZena (m. George Purnell and Joseph Waters) of Cape May, NJ; Olive (m. Charles Cooper and Archie Waters) of Cape May, NJ; and Drucilla (m. James Robinson and Samuel Allen) of Cape May, NJ--has descendants who share significant DNA amounts that prove their relationship with the Plater and Keene family.

Current OFCCCIA membership does not include anyone living with the surname of Plater. The last descendant of George and Mother Plater and Plater to carry the name was Clifton Alexander Plater (1905-1986). He was the only son of Palestine Plater (Beverly Stock Club charter member) and his wife, Martha (née Dixon). Clifton had one child, a daughter, Sylvia.

Palestine Plater was the stepfather to Martha's son, William David Vaughn (the grandson of the man for whom Vaughn Chapel is named). In addition to Clifton, he and Martha had five daughters together: Rosie, Beatrice, Martha, Elsie, and Mildred. Palestine's sister Rachel had a son, James Alexander Plater (1912-74), who carried on the name. It is believed that the WWII Navy veteran died without any surviving children.[108]

The scarcity of Black people with the Plater surname in Dorchester County prior to 1840, along with the active slave traders who resided at Sotterley Plantation in St. Mary's County, suggests that George Plater's parents were in Southern Maryland. It is a strong possibility, as it is with Harriet Tubman, whose grandparents were transported from Africa, that both George Plater's parents came directly from Africa, and his direct descendants did not receive any European ethnic traits.

Along with Plater, other European family surnames in the region are also common to Oldfield's Black descendants: namely Banks, Bayley/Bailey, Cornish, Dixon, Ennals, Goldsborough, Henry, Keene, Lake, LeCompte, Linthicum, Mace, Marine, Ross, Stanley, Travers, Tubman, Vickers, and Woolford. European arrivals were mostly English noblemen, but some had Irish, Welsh, and Scottish heritage.[109] DNA test results from this writer reflect a near-negligible range of Welsh and Scottish origin attributable to ancestors from Oldfield.

Connecting to Cousin Harriet

In Dorchester County's Black circles, a running joke is that everyone is a cousin to everyone else, including Harriet Tubman. Even though she did not have children, Harriet (Ross) Tubman had nine siblings, providing fertile ground for the cousin claims to take root.

A never-before published assertion by Oldfield descendants claim a first-cousin relationship with Harriet Tubman by way of an aunt. They identify the wife of Oldfield's John Nichols as Benjamin Ross's sister (also named Harriet). For some of Oldfield's legacy residents, this is where the winning genealogical lottery ticket to Dorchester County's most acclaimed historical figure is claimed.

Harriet and John Nichols had eight children, according to family reports. Census records from 1860 reflect their adult children as two USCT veterans, Virgil (c1825-78) and Garrison (c1838-66). Oral history includes Gabriel (c 1836-1890) and Beverly School trustee James (c1830-85) as their siblings.[110]

Through various oral historical accounts, descendants of Virgil (presumably Harriet Tubman's first cousin) and his wife, Mary Ann (née Driver), have passed along the tradition that they are cousins of Harriet Tubman.[111] Records show that Virgil (1825-1878) and Mary Ann (1833-1923) had eight children in Oldfield village, six of whom lived to adulthood.

"My mom used to talk to me about [our familial relationship to Harriet Tubman], but back then you didn't pay attention to all of that stuff," said Dr. Dean Smith. The last family reunion of the Nichols descendants was in 2009, when over 100 people attended in Cambridge. Their ancestor, Virgil Nichols, was a pastor at Christ Rock Church, where he is buried.

Beyond solidifying their common relatives as John and Harriet Nichols, DNA connections have not corroborated a genetic link to Harriet Tubman, because those DNA samples are not publicly available. Nonetheless, through the Nichols line, surnames related to Harriet Tubman via the relationship of the woman believed was her aunt are: Bazemore, Haywood, Harris, Kiah, King, Long, Opher, Pinder, Queen, Stiles, and Young.

Other surnames commonly associated with being a close relative to Harriet Tubman are: Bowley, Cornish, Greene, Jolley, and Keene. Further, in 1944, on the occasion of the christening of the SS *Harriet Tubman,* the *Afro-American* newspaper printed twenty-two names of relatives in attendance. Their surnames were: Alfred, Blousina, Bryant, Diet, Frazier, Northrup, Proctor, Richardson, Whalen, Wilkins, and Winston. [112]

Tracing the maternal line is the most difficult for genealogists using traditional documentary methods. Crowdsourcing publicly available DNA results would be a game-changer. Until then, we are reliant upon details firsthand accounts provided in the 1869 biography on Harriet Tubman written by Sarah Bradford and later other historians.[113]

Joyce Stokes Jones recalled as a young girl studying slavery in school her mother told her that Harriet Tubman was known to her as simply "Aunt Harriet." As a great-great-grandniece of the woman who spent her later years in Auburn, NY, Jones spent decades collecting oral history from her family members who often visited with "Aunt Harriet." Jones' maternal grandmother was one of Harriet Tubman's favorite grandnieces. Her research into her maternal line showed Harriet's grandmother's name was Modesty who arrived in Maryland from Ghana, West Africa. Modesty's daughter (with an unknown white man) was Harriet's mother (known as Rit), Jones wrote.[114]

"I realized that the people closest to me had a relationship with the greatest heroine in American history. My mother's parents, her siblings[...] were the very same people that Harriet Tubman loved and called family," wrote Jones.

European Connection

Descriptions of skin color for manumitted Black people in Dorchester most often suggest that they did not have European ancestry. Additionally, Oldfield's oral history captured to date does not reflect an acknowledgment of European heritage. In the case of the ancestors of this author who helped settle Oldfield, surprisingly, it does not appear (conclusively via DNA) that sexual violence against Black women resulted in known offspring.

In Kate Clifford Larson's biography of Harriet Tubman, *Bound for the Promised Land*, she asserts that "Tubman's story begins with the history of some of the white families who claimed ownership of her and her family." Along with the white Pattisons, Thompsons, Stewarts, and Brodess's she notes that Ezekial Keene and his children, Samuel and Anna, inherited members of Harriet's family. In contrast, this writer asserts that Tubman's story begins not with the paperwork of ownership by enslavers, but with the tireless nearly invisible reunification efforts of close relatives of Tubman's parents. Despite the difficulty of identifying familiar relationships with a paper trail, Harriet herself would have likely approve of descendants amplifying narratives that link her to displaced aunts, uncles and cousins knowing that in her own lifetime such relationships were extremely difficult to maintain.

Black Keenes of Dorchester

One of Oldfield's statesmen, Rev. Charles Keene, and his wife Lucinda (née Henry), both born circa 1820, around the same time as Harriet Tubman, had five sons and nine daughters. Unlike Harriet, Charles was born free. Certificate of freedom records depict Charles ("of high chestnut color") as the twenty-two-year-old son of Ann Keene (born circa 1790), who was freed by Roger Jones prior to her son's birth.[115]

Genealogical research is rife with spelling variations, and in this case, with Kane, Cain, and Keen, even though they all link to the Keene family—a nonexistent roadblock with the advent of DNA mapping. Although Charles's surname is spelled differently at times, DNA analysis proves that both he and Lucinda are this author's third great-grandparents.

One would be hard-pressed to find one descendant of Oldfield's founding families who is not related to the Keenes either by blood or by marriage. Endogamy practices were rare because the Black Keenes were not encouraged to marry first or second cousins. However, it was common in the Black community to see multiple marriages between two non-related families.

In addition, there are instances where two brothers of one family married two sisters of another, resulting in creating double first cousins for their children. Such is the case with this writer's great-grandmother, Lillie Plater, and her sister Olive Plater, who married brothers, Greenwood Waters and Archie Waters, respectively. The descendants of Archie and Olive "Ollie" Waters' daughter, Florence M. Waters (1918-96), and her husband, Kenneth Stewart (1916-89) of New Jersey, are double cousins to this writer.

A third Plater sister, Alex Zena (sometimes Alexzena), married and had a son (Leon) with Joseph Waters of Maryland, and DNA analysis suggests Joseph is a close relative of Greenwood and Archie, likely a first cousin. Such occurrences must be considered when evaluating DNA results, as some may assume a closer relationship than is true based on large amounts of shared genetic material.

The descendants of Charles and Lucinda's grandson, Palestine Plater (1875–1960), can claim a relationship with the majority of the current membership of the OFCCCIA either by blood or marriage.

Harriet Tubman's Baltimore Family of Keenes

Not unlike the Nichols family, the Keene family out of Baltimore report via oral history of their close familial relationship with Harriet Tubman. The Baltimore Afro American scooped news outlets in 1944 on the occasion of a ship dedication named in honor of Harriet Tubman with the inclusion of a family of Keenes who migrated to Baltimore by 1900 from the Blackwater region in Dorchester County.

Above - Front row (L to R): Kevin Thomas, Marie K. Stewart, Marshall C. Booze III, Vanise T. Joy, Bertha M. Briscoe. Back row (L to R): Marshal C. Booze Jr. Corp. Jonathan Booze, Bertram Keene, Anita Stewart, Annabelle Cherry, Charles Keene, Anthony Booze, Louise Keene, Lucia Wright, Contance Thomas, Dorothy Booze.

Courtesy of the AFRO American Newspapers Archives/Afro Charities

Sitting in front of her birthday cake Marie (Keene) Stewart (1896-1975) with her brother Charles Keene (1910-78), standing behind her, the pair of siblings have long claimed to be relatives of Harriet Tubman in multiple news accounts spanning decades. Marie and her husband Charles Stewart (not pictured) along with their three daughters Dorothy Keene, Anita Stewart, and Viola Stewart kept 830 N. Bond St. as their family home for generations.

Marie and Charles' parents are George L. Keene (1865-1936) and the former Johanna Hughes (1872-1932) of Dorchester County. Their brother, George A. Keene, also reported that he was related to the Tubman family via their paternal lineage. Research into the Baltimore Keenes' ancestry hit a brick wall. Keene is a popular name, and it has not yet been determined which Keene family in lower Dorchester County are their grandparents. Unlocking the mystery could rest with comparing DNA shared by the known descendants of Tubmans's siblings, which is not yet publicly available. However, we must continue to respect the time-honored tradition of oral history as families continue to reconcile the painful separation of family members over generations.

Encountering Genealogical Brick Walls

Tracing Black families prior to the Civil War (whether free or enslaved) is difficult; identifying women and girls on publicly available genealogical records before they married is nearly impossible.

Case in point, Rev. Charles Keene's certificate of freedom identifies his mother, Ann, as free in 1819 when he was born. There is no additional paper trail for Ann, likely born near the turn of the century, and researchers encounter a brick wall. With the advent of DNA testing, researchers have been able to chip away at that brick wall.

While no certificate of freedom was found, this writer's third great-grandmother, Lucinda, is listed as a free inhabitant on the 1850 census along with her husband and children. On several of their children's death certificates, Lucinda's maiden name of Henry was provided, which makes death certificates a helpful research tool for uncovering maternal lines.

The 1820 through 1850 census enumerated only the heads of household. John Henson Henry (c. 1790–1885), born a generation earlier than Lucinda, is listed as a free man, but there are no government birth or death records in the county prior to 1890. Family bibles, church records, and military records can be great resources. Luckily, Henson Henry's known descendants share enough DNA with descendants of Lucinda that it is likely that he was her father (or a slight chance he is her uncle).

Hypothesizing that Henson Henry is Lucinda's father, she had two brothers: Henson Henry (m. Mary Keene), with eight children, and John Henry (m. Rachel Montgomery), with four children. Lucinda's sister and one sister, Milcah "Milkey" Henry (m. John Small Sr.), with seven children. There is still satisfaction in solving a thousand-piece puzzle even if there are ten pieces missing.

Breaking the DNA Code

Submitting DNA is not without risks, and the decision should be informed and made with a sober mind. Uncovering unexpected paternity results can unlock more trauma and upend family relationships. The personal decision is not the same as an individual choice. The DNA that is unique to each person does not belong only to that person. We each carry aspects passed along from our parents, grandparents, and so on.

When more people submit their DNA, the comparative sample sizes increase. As technology improves, we may have enough data that loosens a full brick from the wall that shields us from our African and Native American history.

Periodically, Ancestry.com's algorithms are updated to reallocate percentages of origin. Having tests from siblings a generation older allows me to make some informed hypotheses about the path taken to Oldfield, but they are not conclusive. The primary geographical regions of Grandma Calvert's ancestors are a variety of West African ethnicities (a broad and predictable determination) that include Ghana, Ivory Coast, Nigeria, Mali, Senegal, and the Bantu peoples.

A genealogical find is to uncover the name of the enslaver who bequeathed our ancestors to their heirs, like they did cattle, watches, and land, but it is not the beginning of our origin story. We must resist attempts to reframe our struggles, resilience and mere existence through a Eurocentric lens.

Although we are far removed from our cousins across the Atlantic, our healing comes from embracing the fractured customs and preserving the piecemeal history of our ancestors in this foreign land. Seeing ourselves in the face of others reaffirms that what is understood does not need to be spoken.

In Closing

Not only has the living not been easy, but to have Black people's lived experiences challenged, if not erased altogether can be soul-depleting. Personal genealogy gathering has been the Black family's survival guide. What historically has been captured by story and song can now be mapped to our DNA. With advent of genetic sequencing, we have a pathway and opportunity to stand in solidarity with our Native friends and family.

In a move towards reconciliation, Nanticoke Historic Preservation Alliance (NHPA) obtained grant funding from the National Parks Service to open the Three Cultures Center on the site of what once was a sprawling native American community called Chicone Village. The Center is designed to educate the public, through living history events, on the history of three cultures: Indigenous people, European settlers and those of African descent who have lived in the Nanticoke River region of the Eastern Shore.

NHPA's work includes protecting local artifacts from being sold internationally. The organization was instrumental in erecting a memorial marker on Dorchester County's Handsell plantation to honor the indigenous people who lived there 2,500 years before it became a site of horrific abuses that accompanied laws that permit forced labor.[116]

The historical relevance of sites where Black and indigenous communities lived and converged has been overlooked by systems designed to maintain their oppression. Data compiled by Maryland Historical Trust evaluated close to 15,000 of the state's archaeological sites recorded, of which a lowly 549 have an African ethnic association. Of counties, Anne Arundel has the greatest number, 127, followed by Prince George's 79, Baltimore City has 38, while Dorchester has 13.[117]

The ebbs and flow of progress, inclusion, and recognition are evident in the interrogation into the life led by Harriet Tubman and her family at the site of her birthplace. Research began in 2021 on the ten acres that were once the home of Harriet Tubman's family. At the site prone to flooding, archeologists uncovered several mid-19th century artifacts as well as an 1808 coin (the year Harriet's parents were married). The terrain "threatens to wash away pieces of history."

> As a society, we predominantly study history from written accounts. In doing so, however, we ignore the rich histories of people whose stories may have never reached the page. Enslaved people were largely illiterate, forcibly kept from written language by slave masters who sought to deprive them of education in order to avoid potential uprisings.
>
> –Sydney Giuliano US Fish and Wildlife, 2025

In a 2024 state needs-assessment report, the findings were that standard methodologies used found "many African American sites as 'insignificant' [...]" and because white evaluators determine "potential importance through a lens of race," they conclude that Black communities are "less likely identified or determined eligible, for historic significance.[118]

As marginalized communities, people of African and Native American ancestry encounter similar resistance when it comes to breaking through genealogical brick walls, but the labor continues. Ella Fitzgerald along with Louis Armstrong's orchestra captured the enduring optimism in the opening lines of the Porgy and Bess classic:

"Summertime and the living is easy":

One of these mornings
You're gonna rise up singing
Yes, you'll spread your wings
And you'll take to the sky
But 'til that mornin'
There's nothin' can harm you[119]

Fueled by faith, finding optimism was nonetheless a struggle. The ancestors sat up straight when the country's first Black president, Barack Obama, in his second term, authorized a National Monument to honor Harriet Tubman in Church Creek that includes a byway of historical sites, a visitor center, and a museum[120] A decade later, in May 2025, Maryland's first Black governor, Wes Moore, vetoed legislation deemed essential for the movement towards reparations, and the ancestors likely dropped their heads. As the saying goes, all skin-folk, ain't kinfolk.

Countless Africans landed on Maryland's Eastern Shore, stolen people on stolen land. Every day since has been a conscious choice to survive and build community. Each gathering, large or small, is a reminder that we are our ancestors' wildest dreams. As sons and daughters of kings and queens, we must remember to hold their memories in reverence and find purpose knowing their sacrifices led to our opportunities.

"If you are silent about your pain, they'll kill you and say you enjoyed it."

— Zora Neale Hurston

L to R from top: Dr. Melissa Glee McGuire and Monica R. J. Bland (2024). George Wiley (c. 1960). Maurice "Mo" Vaughn and Victor Harris Vaughan (2007). Courtesy Victor Harris Vaughan. Calmetta Brinkley (2024). Courtesy OFCCCIA.

"[Enslaved Blacks] would tell their children what happened to them in their lifetime. And if their child did not survive to tell me or the generation after that, then all of that's lost. So I still think that survival is most important."

—Agnes Kane Callum (1925-2015), historian, author, founder of Baltimore Afro-American Historical and Genealogical Society

L to R from top: Calvert Wiley (c. 1970). John H. Wiley, Jr. Tony Johnson, John H. Wiley (2015). Broderick Patterson Jr. and his grandfather John H. Wiley Jr. Theresa Wiley and Deborah (Wiley) Davis (c. 1975). Photos courtesy of Keesha Ha.

L to R Rhonda Wiley Fields and Sanda (Wiley) Eaton, front row. Calvert Moore and Rowan Ha.
Yolanda (Wiley) Conyers, Ebony Harris, Monica Osbourne and Keesha (Lawson, Patterson) Ha.

Acknowledgements

Immense gratitude is extended to the community of genealogists as well as close and distant family members for their love,support, and inspiration: Adisa and Amy Griffin, Latayna, Dennis, and Dequan Nelson, Rosalind Jackson, Vanessa Gordon, Rosalie Jackson, Erma McDuffie, Gary March, Deborah Davis, Sarah Wiley, Clifford Wiley, Brent Wiley, Charles Payne, Jamel Green, Dr. Pam Holman, and my cousin-twin, Monica R. J. Bland. This road may not have been ever traveled without the guidance of godmother and librarian at The Historic Samuel Coleridge Taylor Elementary School in West Baltimore, the late Juliet (née Burns) Carter (and first cousin to the late U.S. Supreme Court Chief Justice Thurgood Marshall).

The seed for this book was planted during the 2023-24 planning for the 130th anniversary of the rebuilding of the historic Vaughn Chapel in Oldfield. Members of the Oldfield Church Creek Community Improvement Association including then-president William Jarmon along with Vic Vaughan, Dr. Dean Smith, Sam Opher, David Vaughn, Gloria Woolford, and Joe Henry were all central to it taking root. The graciousness and guidance of Calmetta Brinkley became the nurturing elements that brought this book to fruition.

Behind the scenes, a nod of gratitude to Tracy Chiles McGhee, Jessica Layman, and Rona Kobell for always rising to the occasion and to the sisterhood of writers at Zora's Den, with Victoria Adams-Kennedy as the inspirational muse, who shined brightly during each season until time of harvest. A special nod to Harriet Tubman scholar Kate Clifford Larson for her generosity of time and expertise. Furthermore, this book would not be possible without the best hype man ever and Gloria Richardson biographer, Joseph R. Fitzgerald. Thank you for inviting me into the community of writers and storytellers, but most importantly the constant reminder that the struggle is indeed eternal.

Forever grateful,
Keesha

In Loving Memory

CALVERT (WATERS) WILEY

1913-1982

Daughter of Greenwood Waters (*Princess Anne*, MD) and Lillie Plater (*Church Creek*, MD)

Mother of Edward Ball, Russell Wiley, Katherine (Wiley) Lunkin, Ella Louise (Wiley) Jones, John H. Wiley Jr, William Wiley, Walter Wiley, Sarah Wiley, Phyllis (Wiley) Carter, Gilbert Wiley, and Joseph Wiley of Baltimore

Wife of John Wiley Sr

Sister of Leroy, Joseph, Russell, William, Franklin, Thomas, Louise (Lee), Evelyn (Harriday), Lillie (West) and Mildred (Dixon) Waters

Granddaughter of Alexander Plater and Louisa Keene
Great granddaughter of Charles Keene and Lucinda Henry

Calvert (Waters) Wiley, my grandmother, whose lesser-known story sheds light on the path that connects us to the land of Harriet Tubman.

Appendix

POPULATION OF MARYLAND.

1830.

	Whites.	Free Blacks.	Slaves.
The Whole State...............	291,108	52,938	102,994

1860.

Counties.	Whites.	Free Blacks.	Slaves.
Allegany	27,215	467	666
Anne Arundel....................	11,704	4,864	7,332
Baltimore County...............	46,722	4,231	3,182
City of Baltimore...............	184,520	25,680	2,218
Calvert	3,997	1,841	4,609
Caroline..........................	7,604	2,786	739
Carroll...........................	22,525	1,225	783
Cecil	19,994	2,918	950
Charles...........................	5,796	1,068	9,653
Dorchester	11,654	4,684	4,123
Frederick.........................	38,391	4,957	3,243
Harford...........................	17,971	3,644	1,800
Howard...........................	9,081	1,395	2,862
Kent..............................	7,347	3,411	2,509
Montgomery	11,349	1,552	5,421
Prince George's.................	9,650	1,198	12,479
Queen Anne's....................	8,415	3,372	4,174
St. Mary's.......................	6,798	1,866	6,549
Somerset..........................	15,332	4,571	5,089
Talbot............................	8,106	2,964	3,725
Washington.......................	28,305	1,677	1,435
Worcester	13,442	3,571	3,648
The Whole State........	515,918	83,942	87,189

Chart 1 – Maryland's free and enslaved population

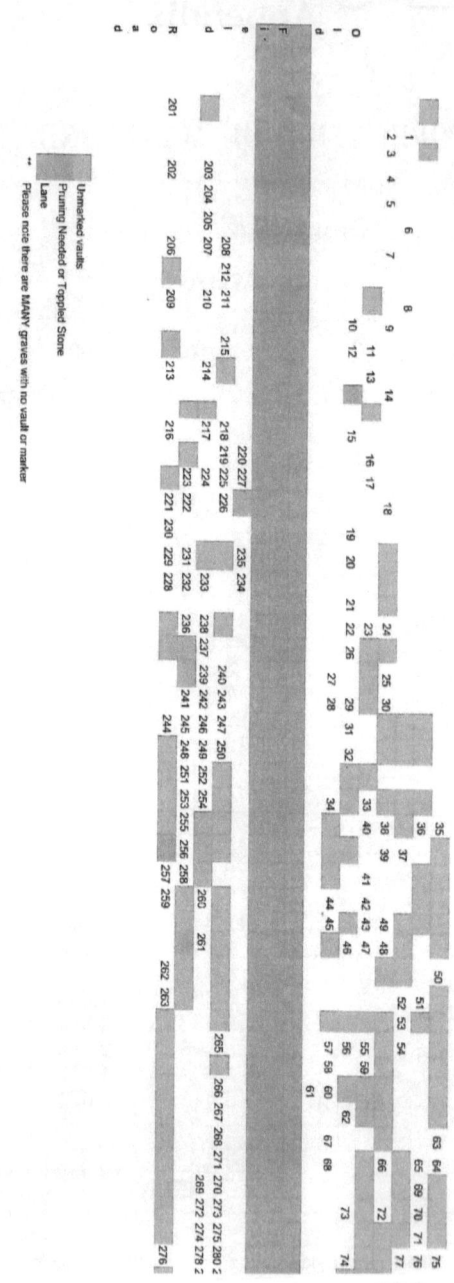

Chart 2- Oldfield Cemetery's partial list of burials

What a Story to Tell the Children

Rachel J Farrow

⊹ancestry

Descendancy

1. Rachel J Farrow b: Abt. 1820 in Dorchester County, Maryland, USA. d: 22 Jan 1929 in Church Creek Cambridge Do, Maryland, USA; age: 109.
+ George Plater b: Abt. 1820 in Dorchester County, Maryland, USA. d: 1880 in MARYLAND USA; age: 60.
   2. Alexander Plater b: 5 May 1851 in Dorchester County, Maryland, USA. d: 5 Apr 1912 in Church Creek Dorchester County, Maryland, USA; age: 60.
   + Louisa Jane Keene b: 9 Oct 1848 in Dorchester County, Maryland, USA. m: 1874. d: 16 May 1916 in Church Creek Dorchester Maryland, USA; age: 67.
      3. Palestine S Plater b: 10 Aug 1875 in Maryland. d: 5 May 1960 in Maryland, USA; age: 84.
      + Martha Dixon b: 6 Apr 1878 in Church Creek, Dorchester, Maryland, USA. d: Dec 1956 in Maryland, USA; age: 78.
         4. William David Vaughn b: 29 Sep 1901 in Church Creek, Maryland, USA. d: 28 March 1980 in Cambridge, Dorchester, Maryland, USA; age: 78.
         + Ella B b: abt 1902 in Maryland. d: Deceased.
         + Cecelia Salem Hughes b: 12 Feb 1907 in Maryland USA. d: 11 Feb 1945 in Maryland, USA; age: 37.
         4. Clifton Alexander Plater b: 7 Mar 1905 in Maryland. d: Jul 1986 in Cambridge, Dorchester, Maryland, USA; age: 81.
         + Mary b: abt 1912 in Maryland. d: Deceased.
         4. Rosie Louise Plater b: Sep 1906 in Maryland. d: Jan 1927 in Maryland, USA; age: 20.
         + Samuel James Benjamin Harris b: Abt. 1903 in Church Creek, Dorchester, Maryland, USA. d: Deceased.
         4. Beatrice Olivia Plater b: abt 1909 in Church Creek Dorchester Maryland, USA. d: Aft. 1945; age: 36.
         + Rudell Humane b: 13 Feb 1903 in Cambridge, Maryland, USA. d: 18 August 1947; age: 44.
         4. Martha Selena Plater b: 18 Mar 1910 in Maryland. d: 23 Nov 1987 in Cambridge, Dorchester, Maryland, USA; age: 77.
         + Harold Floyd Perry b: 27 Jun 1911 in Bucktown, Maryland, USA. d: Deceased in Cambridge, Dorchester County, Maryland, United States of America.
         4. Elsie Elizabeth Plater b: 5 Aug 1915 in Dorchester County Maryland, USA. d: 2 Oct 1941 in Dorchester County Maryland, USA; age: 26.
         4. Mildred Plater b: 21 Sept 1917 in Church Creek, Dorchester, Maryland, USA. d: 18 Aug 2016 in Dorcester, Maryland, USA; age: 98.
         + Philip Lee Hughes b: Jan 1911 in Maryland. d: 19 Feb 1976 in Maryland; age: 65.
         4. George Plater b: abt 1919 in Cambridge Maryland, USA. d: 1950 in Baltimore Maryland, USA; age: 31.
      3. Wilhemena Willie Plater b: Jan 1876 in Dorcester, Maryland, USA. d: Dec 1936 in Cambridge Dorchester County, Maryland, USA; age: 60.
      + Jason Benjamin Henry b: 1 Apr 1874 in Cambridge, Dorchester, Maryland, USA. m: 1897. d: 26 Sep 1956 in Cambridge, Dorchester, Maryland, USA; age: 82.
         4. Claude Plater Henry b: 3 Mar 1899 in Cambridge, Dorchester, Maryland, USA. d: 1940 in Pennsylvania, USA; age: 40.
         + Margaret Annie Woolford b: 1901 in Maryland. m: 26 Dec 1918 in Dorchester County, Maryland. d: 1931 in Cambridge, Dorchester, Maryland, USA; age: 30.
         4. Louise Henry b: abt 1901 in Maryland. d: 1978; age: 77.
         + James Smith b: Maryland, USA. d: Deceased.
         4. Aurelia "Ruth" W Henry b: 1 Jul 1902 in Cambridge, Dorchester, Maryland, USA. d: 29 December 1972 in Baltimore Maryland, USA; age: 70.
         + Wilbur Charles Jackson b: 13 Aug 1898 in Bucktown, Maryland, USA. d: 17 Nov 1954 in Greeg, Union, Pennsylvania, USA; age: 56.
         4. Mary Rachel Henry b: 23 May 1904 in Dorchester County, Maryland, USA. m: 24 Oct 1922. d: 5 Nov 2005 in Cambridge, Dorchester, Maryland; age: 101.
         + Wilbert James Woolford Rev b: 21 Sep 1898 in Cambridge, Dorchester, Maryland, USA. m: 24 Oct 1922. d: 21 Aug 1983 in Cambridge, Dorchester, Maryland, USA; age: 84.
         4. Martha Henry b: 22 July 1906 in Dorchester County, Maryland, United States of America. d: 7 February 1989 in Maryland, United States of America; age: 82.
         + Milton H Vaughn Rev b: 2 Feb 1901 in Cambridge, Dorchester County, Maryland, United States of America. d: December 1975 in Baltimore City, Maryland, United States of America; age: 74.
         4. Clara Elizabeth Henry b: 7 Feb 1909 in Church Creek, Maryland. d: 23 Aug 1998 in Baltimore, Baltimore City, Maryland, USA; age: 89.
         + Charles William Stills Sr. b: 7 Oct 1906 in Callands, Pittsylvania County, Virginia. m: 1932. d: 12 Nov 1969 in Maryland; age: 63.
         4. James Alexander Henry b: 23 Apr 1910 in Church Creek, Maryland, USA. d: Aug 1965 in Wilmington, New Castle, Delaware, USA; age: 55.
         + Grace Wheatley b: 13 March 1903 in Dorchester County, Maryland, USA. d: 26 March 1969 in Delaware; age: 66.
         4. Lettie G Henry b: 11 Aug 1911 in Cambridge, Dorchester, Maryland, USA. d: 15 Apr 1975 in Baltimore Md. USA; age: 63.
         + Garfield Henry b: 7 May 1903 in Cambridge, Maryland, USA. d: 13 Jan 1986; age: 82.
         + Miller b: Abt. 1910 in Maryland, USA. d: Deceased.
         4. Wilhelmina Willie Henry b: 14 Feb 1913 in Cambridge, Maryland. d: 13 Mar 1996 in Philadelphia, Philadelphia, Pennsylvania, USA; age: 83.
         + John R Hickson b: abt 1884 in USA. m: 1938 in New Jersey, USA. d: Abt. 1965 in Philadelphia Pennsylvania; age: 81.
         4. Rebecca Rosealie Henry b: 7 Jun 1914 in Maryland. d: 16 May 1990 in Bronx, Bronx, New York, USA; age: 75.
         + Lewis E Taylor b: 1 November 1906 in Pennsylvania, USA. d: 25 October 1985 in Brooklyn, Kings, New York, USA; age: 78.
      3. William Plater b: Abt. 1879 in Dorchester County, Maryland, USA. d: Bef. 1945 in Maryland, USA; age: 66.
      + Ida J Woodland b: abt 1892 in Maryland. d: Abt. 1935 in Maryland, USA; age: 43.
         4. Joseph Edward Plater b: 4 Apr 1911 in St Mary's, Maryland, USA. d: Deceased in Maryland, USA.
         + Louise A Clark b: 6 Jun 1905 in Maryland, USA. d: 7 Jun 2002 in Maryland; age: 97.
         4. Sarah Agnes Plater b: abt 1913 in Maryland. d: Deceased.
         + William Woodland b: abt 1915 in Maryland. d: Deceased.
         4. Rosanna Plater b: abt 1915 in Maryland. d: Deceased.
         4. James Cornelius Plater b: 8 Oct 1915 in St Mary's County, Maryland, USA. d: 2 Oct 1973 in Berkeley, West Virginia; age: 57.
         + Ada M b: abt 1919 in North Carolina. d: Deceased.

4. Robert S Plater b: abt 1918 in St Mary's County, Maryland, USA. d: Deceased.
4. Alice Plater b: abt 1919 in Maryland. d: Deceased.
4. William Plater b: 10 May 1920 in Charles, Maryland, USA. d: Deceased.
4. John Henry Plater b: 11 May 1924 in St Mary's, Maryland, USA. d: Deceased.
4. Mary Frances Plater b: 25 Dec 1925 in Charles County, Maryland, USA. d: 16 Jan 1990; age: 64.
+ Joseph S Goldring b: abt 1920 in Maryland. d: Deceased.
3. Rachel A Plater b: 07 Aug 1881 in Beverly, Dorchester County, Maryland, USA. d: 22 Nov 1959 in Philadelphia, Pennsylvania, USA; age: 78.
+ Charles Henry Payne b: 22 Mar 1879 in Goochland, Virginia, USA. d: 24 Mar 1955 in Philadelphia, Philadelphia, Pennsylvania, USA; age: 76.
    4. James Alexander Plater b: 03 Apr 1912 in Pennsylvania. d: 7 Sep 1974 in Dade, Florida, United States; age: 62.
    + Grace Emma Melvina Blackledge b: 02 Sep 1914 in Philadelphia, PA. m: 15 Sep 1936 in Cape May, New Jersey. d: 20 Apr 2006 in Kendall Park, Middlesex, New Jersey; age: 91.
    4. Mildred Ardella Payne b: 23 Aug 1915 in Cambridge, Dorchester, Maryland, USA. d: 17 Jun 2015 in North Cape May, New Jersey, USA; age: 99.
    + James Alexander "DUCK" Moore b: 4 Jun 1905. d: 29 Jan 1998 in Middle Township, Cape May, New Jersey, USA; age: 92.
    4. William Alfred "Brother" Payne b: 08 Sep 1917 in Cambridge, Dorchester, Maryland, USA. d: 17 Jun 2009 in Wyncote, Pa; age: 91.
    + Margaret Josephine Parker b: 18 Feb 1924 in King and Queen County, Virginia. m: 16 Jul 1944 in Philadelphia, Pennsylvania. d: 19 Nov 2015 in Philadelphia, PA; age: 91.
    4. Charles Melvin Payne Sr. b: 22 Feb 1921 in Cambridge, Dorchester, Maryland, USA. d: 16 Aug 1990 in Woodbine, Cape May, New Jersey, USA; age: 69.
    + Beatrice Smith b: 1 Jan 1925 in Atlantic City, Atlantic, New Jersey, USA. m: 29 Jun 1947 in Woodbine, New Jersey. d: 17 Apr 2012 on Cape May Court House, Cape May, New Jersey, USA; age: 87.
3. Lillie W Plater b: 3 May 1883 in Church Creek Cambridge Do, Maryland, USA. d: 13 Mar 1949 in Baltimore, Maryland, USA; age: 65.
+ Greenwood N Waters b: 05 Apr 1876 in Somerset County, Maryland, USA. m: 20 Dec 1899 in Dorchester, Maryland, United States. d: 27 Nov 1952 in Baltimore, Maryland, USA; age: 76.
    4. Mabel Waters b: May 1900 in Cambridge, Dorchester, Maryland, USA. d: Deceased in Maryland , USA.
    4. Wilhemena Willie Waters b: 25 May 1902 in Dorchester County Maryland, USA. d: Deceased.
    4. Leroy Elious Waters b: 29 Jan 1903 in Baltimore, Baltimore Independent, Maryland, United States. d: 27 Oct 1990 in Baltimore, Baltimore, Maryland, United States; age: 87.
    + Sarah C Jackson b: abt 1907 in Virginia. m: 1926. d: 1955; age: 48.
    + Frances b: Abt. 1910. d: Abt. 1995 in Baltimore Maryland, USA; age: 85.
    4. Louise Plater Waters b: 28 Oct 1906 in Baltimore, Maryland. d: Dec 1978 in maryland, usa, or, Pennsylvania, USA; age: 72.
    + Elzie Elsie Henry Jones b: 7 Apr 1901 in Deal Island, Maryland, USA. d: Deceased.
    + James Lee b: abt 1905. d: Deceased in Maryland.
    4. Joseph Emory Waters b: 25 May 1909 in Baltimore, Baltimore, Maryland, United States. d: Apr 1994 in Maryland, USA; age: 84.
    + Amanda b: Abt. 1913 in Maryland, USA. d: Abt. 1995 in Baltimore Maryland, USA; age: 82.
    4. Russell Waters b: abt 1912 in Baltimore City, Maryland, USA. d: Bef. 1950 in Maryland, USA; age: 38.
    4. Calvert Elisabeth Waters b: 12 Jul 1913 in Baltimore, Baltimore (Independent City), Maryland. d: 8 Dec 1982 in Baltimore, Baltimore City, Maryland, United States of America; age: 69.
    + Edward Delaney Ball b: 2 Jun 1913 in Philadelphia, Philadelphia, Pennsylvania, USA. m: 31 Dec 1931 in Philadelphia, Philadelphia, Pennsylvania, United States. div: 11 Oct 1946 in Virginia, USA. d: 24 Sep 1963 in Washington City, Washington, District of Columbia; age: 50.
    + John Henry Wiley b: 23 Feb 1902 in Baltimore Maryland, USA. m: Aug 1967 in Atlantic, Atlantic, New Jersey, USA. d: Dec 1981 in Baltimore Maryland, USA; age: 79.
    4. William O Waters b: 24 Jun 1915 in Baltimore, Baltimore, Maryland, United States. d: Abt. 1955 in Maryland, USA; age: 39.
    + Gladys H b: abt 1915 in Maryland. d: Deceased.
    4. Franklin Waters b: abt 1918 in Maryland, United States. d: Feb 1942 in Baltimore Maryland, USA; age: 24.
    + Helen b: abt 1918. d: Deceased.
    4. Evelyn Frances Waters b: 29 Jan 1920 in Baltimore, Baltimore, Maryland, United States. d: 15 Mar 1997 in Philadelphia, Pensylvania, USA; age: 77.
    + Harriday b: Abt. 1910 in Maryland. d: Deceased.
    + William "Biggie" Butler b: Abt. 1920 in Maryland, USA. d: Deceased.
    4. Thomas Nelson Waters b: 24 May 1921 in Baltimore, Baltimore, Maryland, United States. d: 27 Jan 2001 in Baltimore, Baltimore, Maryland, United States; age: 79.
    + Willie Mae Armstrong b: abt 1922 in North Carolina. d: Deceased in Maryland, USA.
    4. Lillie Alfreda Waters b: 22 Feb 1923 in Baltimore, Maryland, USA. d: 31 Mar 1987 in Baltimore, Baltimore City, Maryland, USA; age: 64.
    + Brunes West b: 19 Dec 1905 in Saluda South Carolina, USA. m: 4 February 1950 in Baltimore, Maryland, USA. d: 16 Nov 1978 in Baltimore, Baltimore,Maryland,USA; age: 72.
    4. Mildred Waters b: 16 Dec 1924 in Baltimore, Baltimore, Maryland, United States. d: 4 Jul 1988 in Baltimore, Baltimore, Maryland, United States; age: 63.
    + Joseph Dixon b: Abt. 1922. d: Deceased in Maryland, USA.
3. Bethina "Bertha" Glasco Plater b: 29 Mar 1885 in Dorchester County, Maryland, USA. d: 29 Dec 1959 in Cambridge Dorchester County, Maryland, USA; age: 74.
+ Robert Ward Cummings b: 1 Feb 1884 in Maryland. d: 1966 in Baltimore, Baltimore City, Maryland, USA; age: 81.
    4. Edward Alexander Cummings b: 24 Sep 1911 in Maryland. d: Jul 1975 in Hurlock, Dorchester, Maryland, USA; age: 63.
    + Pattie Lee Walker b: 19 Aug 1919 in Mecklenburg County, Virginia . d: 27 Nov 1995 in Dorchester County, Maryland, USA; age: 76.
    4. Robert Gooden Cummings b: 3 Feb 1916 in Baltimore, Maryland, USA. d: July 1981 in Delaware; age: 65.
    + Ada b: abt 1921 in North Carolina. d: Deceased.
    4. Clarence G Cummings b: 21 Sep 1917 in Baltimore, Maryland, USA. d: 25 Jul 1981 in Greenwood, Sussex County, Delaware, United States of America; age: 63.
    + Flora b: Abt. 1920.
    4. Nellie Jane Cummings b: 6 Sep 1918 in Dorchester County, Maryland, USA. d: 22 October 2011 in Milford, Sussex, Delaware, USA; age: 93.
    + Paul Sudler b: 6 Dec 1928 in Woodside, Delaware, USA. m: Abt 1981. d: Deceased.
    + Linton King Sr b: 3 May 1917 in Pennsylvania. d: 14 Nov 1996 in Cambridge, Dorchester, Maryland, USA; age: 79.
    4. Wilmer B Cummings b: 18 Apr 1919 in Maryland, USA. d: Deceased.
    + Cornelia Chew b: 26 Sep 1918 in Croome, Maryland, USA. d: 6 Jun 1995 in Baltimore, Baltimore City, Maryland, USA; age: 76.
3. Alex Zena Plater b: 20 Oct 1886 in Church Creek, Maryland. d: Abt. 1945 in Pennsylvania, USA; age: 58.
+ George William Purnell b: 26 Mar 1883 in Camden, New Jersey, USA. m: 1920 in Philadelphia, Philadelphia, Pennsylvania, USA. d: 21 Nov 1962 in Lyon, New Jersey, USA; age: 79.

4. Helen Louise Purnell b: 11 Jun 1921 in Phila, Pennsylvania. d: 29 Jun 1980 in New Jersey, USA; age: 59.
+ Melvin H Riggs b: 27 Jun 1919 in Camden, New Jersey. d: 4 Jun 1999 in Camden, NJ; age: 79.
4. Elizabeth Zena Purnell b: 1 Nov 1923 in Philadelphia, Philadelphia, Pennsylvania, USA. d: Feb 1994 in Arverne, Queens, New York, USA; age: 70.
+ Charles H Little b: 2 June 1918 in Steubenville, Jefferson, Ohio, USA. m: 1978 in New York City, New York, USA. d: Dec 1978 in Far Rockaway, Queens, New York, USA; age: 60.
+ Thomas Brooks b: 27 Jun 1910 in Harrisburg, Dauphin, Pennsylvania, USA. d: 2 Jan 1998 in Canton, Stark, Ohio, USA; age: 87.
4. George Alexander Purnell b: 3 Mar 1925 in Philadelphia, Pennsylvania. d: 2020; age: 94.
+ Ernestine Hall b: 1930. d: 2020; age: 90.
4. William Edward Purnell b: 23 Nov 1928 in Pennsylvania, USA. d: 2023 in Nebraska, USA; age: 94.
+ Christine b: Oct 1929 in Camden, Camden, New Jersey, USA. d: Oct 2020 in Omaha, Nebraska, USA; age: 91.
+ Joseph Waters b: 1877 in Maryland. d: Deceased.
4. Leon Waters b: 21 Dec 1911 in Philadelphia, Philadelphia, Pennsylvania, USA. d: 25 Feb 1992 in Cape May, Cape May, New Jersey, United States; age: 80.
+ Mabel Andrews b: 11 Jan 1920 in Pennsylvania, USA, . m: 1940 in New Jersey, USA. d: 7 Nov 1978 in Philadelphia, Pennsylvania, USA, ; age: 58.
+ Mary Evalena Williams b: 19 Mar 1917 in Cape May County, New Jersey, USA. d: 14 May 2004 in Colonia, Middlesex, New Jersey, USA; age: 87.
3. Olive Ollie Virginia Plater b: 27 Sep 1888 in Maryland. d: 20 Feb 1968 in Cape May County, New Jersey, USA; age: 79.
+ Charles H. Cooper b: abt 1884 in New Jersey. m: 14 Dec 1907 in Mullica Hill, New Jersey, USA. d: Abt. 1920 in New Jersey, USA; age: 36.
4. Leroy Sylvester Cooper b: 22 May 1908 in Mullica Hill Gloucester, New Jersey, USA. d: 4 Jun 1976 on Cape May Court House, Cape May, New Jersey, USA; age: 68.
+ Gladys Ellen Still b: 7 Jun 1913 in New Jersey. m: 1932 in New Jersey, USA. d: 15 Jan 1986 in Sacramento, Sacramento, California, USA; age: 72.
4. Ida Aurelia Bethena Cooper b: 2 May 1910 in New Jersey. d: 23 Dec 1964 in Philadelphia, Philadelphia, Pennsylvania, USA; age: 54.
+ Grant Bishop b: 15 Nov 1900 in Stockton, Maryland, USA. m: 1934 in Philadelphia, Philadelphia, Pennsylvania, United States. d: 24 Aug 1951 in Philadelphia, Philadelphia, Pennsylvania, USA; age: 50.
+ Spencer Harris b: 14 May 1914. d: Nov 1971 in Chester, Delaware, Pennsylvania, USA; age: 57.
+ Walter Gibson b: 3 Oct 1914. d: Jan 1986 in Pennsylvania, USA; age: 71.
4. Virginia Elsie Cooper b: 15 Jun 1912 in Cape May, New Jersey, USA. d: 19 Jan 1996 in Princeton, Mercer, New Jersey, USA; age: 83.
+ Henry A Gift b: 11 Nov 1911 in Guyana. m: 1954 in Broward, Florida. d: Dec 1997 on Port St. Lucie, FL; age: 86.
+ Samuel Leybrend b: 1910 in North Carolina. div: 1954 in Broward, Florida, USA. d: Deceased.
+ Archie E Waters b: 15 Sep 1888 in Somerset County Maryland, USA. m: 1917 in Philadelphia, Philadelphia, Pennsylvania, United States. d: Jun 1919 in Atlantic, New Jersey, USA; age: 30.
4. Florence Marie Waters b: 9 Jun 1918 in Cape May, Cape May, New Jersey, USA. d: 17 Aug 1996 in Newark, Essex, New Jersey, USA; age: 78.
+ Kenneth Collier Leroy Stewart b: 11/22/1916 in Ridgewood, Bergen, New Jersey, USA. m: 1940 in New Jersey, USA. d: 9 May 1989 in Newark, Essex, New Jersey, USA; age: 72.
3. Drucilla Plater b: 19 Apr 1892 in Maryland. d: 11 Jul 1985 in Middle Township, Cape May, New Jersey, USA; age: 93.
+ Ernest D Hardeman b: 25 Jun 1883 in Alabama, United States. m: 1918 in Philadelphia, Philadelphia, Pennsylvania, United States. d: 2 July 1932 in New York City, New York, USA; age: 49.
+ J James Robinson b: 9 Jun 1882 in Virginia. m: 1924 in Philadelphia, Philadelphia, Pennsylvania, United States. d: 6 Sep 1942 in Pennsylvania; age: 60.
+ Samuel C Allen b: 27 Aug 1883 in Virginia. d: 6 Sep 1942 in Baltimore, Baltimore, Maryland, USA; age: 59.
4. Claude Clendenny Allen b: 10 Oct 1912 in Baltimore, Maryland, USA. d: 1993 in Pennsylvania, USA; age: 80.
+ Olivia b: abt 1920 in Pennsylvania. d: Deceased.
+ Lila Elizabeth Wray b: 5 August 1921 in Wake County, North Carolina, United States of America. d: 17 Mar 1982 in Raleigh, Wake County, North Carolina, United States of America; age: 60.
4. Allen d: Deceased.
2. Carmena Cornelia Plater b: Dec 1855 in Maryland. d: 13 Apr 1914 in Church Creek Dorchester Maryland, USA; age: 58.
+ William Thompson b: Abt. 1855 in Maryland, USA. d: Abt. 1905 in Cambridge Dorchester County, Maryland, USA; age: 50.
3. Florence A Thompson b: 20 Mar 1893 in Dorcester, Maryland, USA. d: Abt. 1983 in Maryland, or, Pennsylvania, USA; age: 89.
+ John Terry b: 7 Jun 1892 in South Carolina. d: Deceased.
2. Mary Ann Plater b: abt 1856 in Church Creek, Dorchester, Maryland, USA. d: Deceased.
2. George E Plater b: Abt. 1857 in Church Creek, Dorchester, Maryland, USA. d: 30 Dec 1935 in Maryland, USA; age: 78.
+ Emma J b: abt 1873 in Maryland. d: Aug 1945 in Dorchester County Maryland, USA; age: 72.
2. William Plater b: 1860 in Church Creek Dorchester County, Maryland, USA. d: Deceased in Maryland, USA.
2. Emma J Plater b: abt 1861 in Dorchester County, Maryland, USA. d: Deceased.
2. mary Plater b: 1861 in Church Creek Dorchester County, Maryland, USA. d: Deceased.
2. Sarah Elizabeth Plater b: Abt 1868 in Dorchester County, Maryland, USA. d: Deceased.

Chart 3 – Mother Plater's descendants' chart

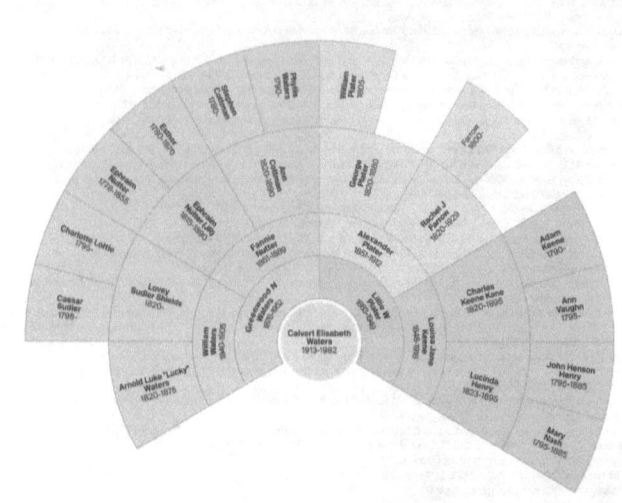

Chart 4 – Grandma Calvert Wiley's family group chart

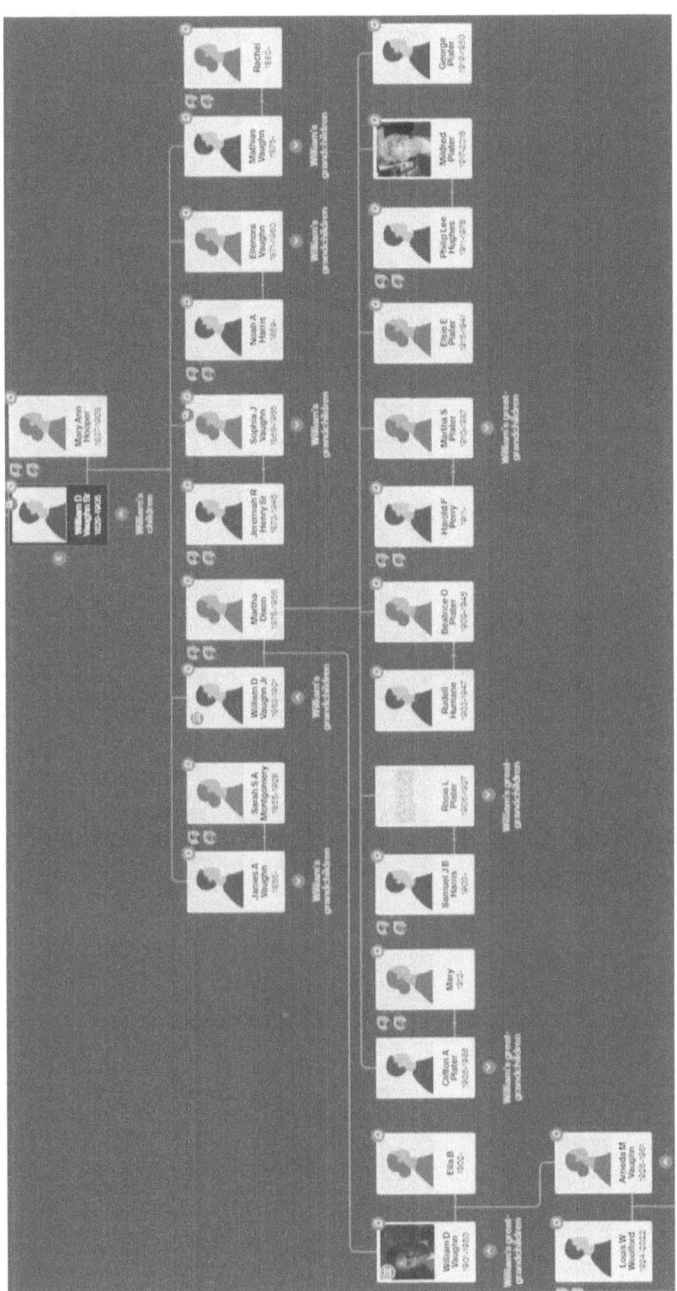

Chart 5 - Rev. Vaughn's family descendants' chart

Oldfield's USCT Veterans

Last Name	First Name	Reg		Last Name	First Name	Reg
Banks	Alexander+o	39		Henry	Jackson°	4
Banks	Benjamin+o	4		Henry	James+o	19
Banks	Benjamin T+o	4		Hughes*	Alexander°	4
Banks	Israel+o	4		Hughes*	William J	4
Banks	James	4		Hughes	William	39
Banks	Jenkins	19		Jarmon	George	19
Banks	Peter+o	4		Jarmon	Isaac°	19
Bryan*	Solomon	4		Jarmon	Rufus+o	19
Camper*	Howard+o	4		Johnson	Joseph°	7
Camper	Stephen+o	39		Kane	Alfred+o	39
Camper*	Stephen H+	4		Kane	Draper	7
Camper	Andrew+o	7		Henry	Jackson	4
Camper	Charles+o	9		Kane	Henry	39
Chase	Charles+o	118		Kane	Josiah+o	4
Cornish	John+o	7/19		Manokey	Thomas J°	39
Cornish*	William H+o	4		Manokey**	Moses	4
Dean	William+o	7		Manoky**	John	4
Dean	William°	19		Marine	Jeremiah°	4
Denby/ Demby	William H°	4		Marine*	John	4
Dixon*	James N+o	4		Montgomery*	John W+o	4
Ennals/ Ennells	Robert+o	39		Montgomery	James	14
Ennels**	William H+o	4		Montgomery	James	39
Ennals/ Ennels*	Josiah+o	4		Opher	Moses+o	19
Fisher*	John+o	4		Plater	Simon°	4
Fisher	John+o	4		Plater	Frisby	7
Harris	Asbury	30		Travers	Henry+o	4
Harris	John	19		Waters	William°	19

Status prior to enlistment   +Invalid or Survivor pension filed
*Free   °Buried at Oldfield
**Enslaved

Chart 6 - Church Creek's USCT veterans

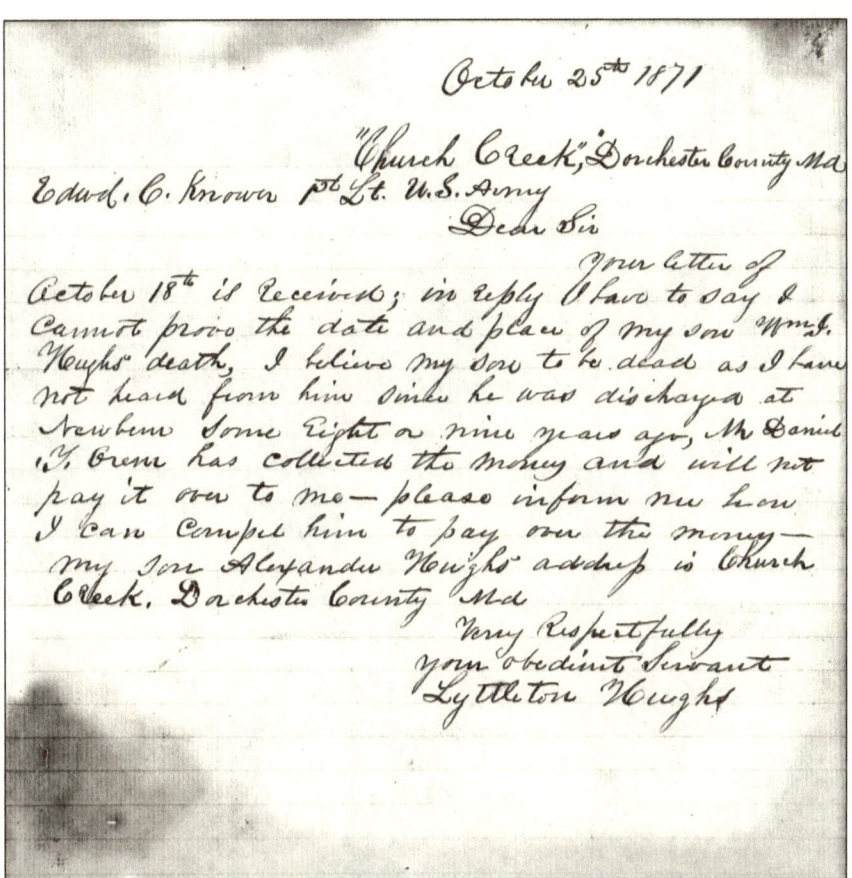

Octob 25th 1871

"Church Creek", Dorchester County Md
Edwd. C. Known 1st Lt. U.S. Army
Dear Sir

Your letter of
October 18th is Received; in reply I have to say I
cannot prove the date and place of my son Wm J.
Hughs death, I believe my son to be dead as I have
not heard from him since he was discharged at
Newbern some eight or nine years ago, Mr Daniel
J. Crem has collected the money and will not
pay it over to me— please inform me how
I can compel him to pay over the money—
my son Alexander Hughs address is Church
Creek, Dorchester County Md
Very Respectfully
your obedient Servant
Lyttleton Hughs

Letter 1 – Littleton Hughes' complaint to Freedmen's Bureau

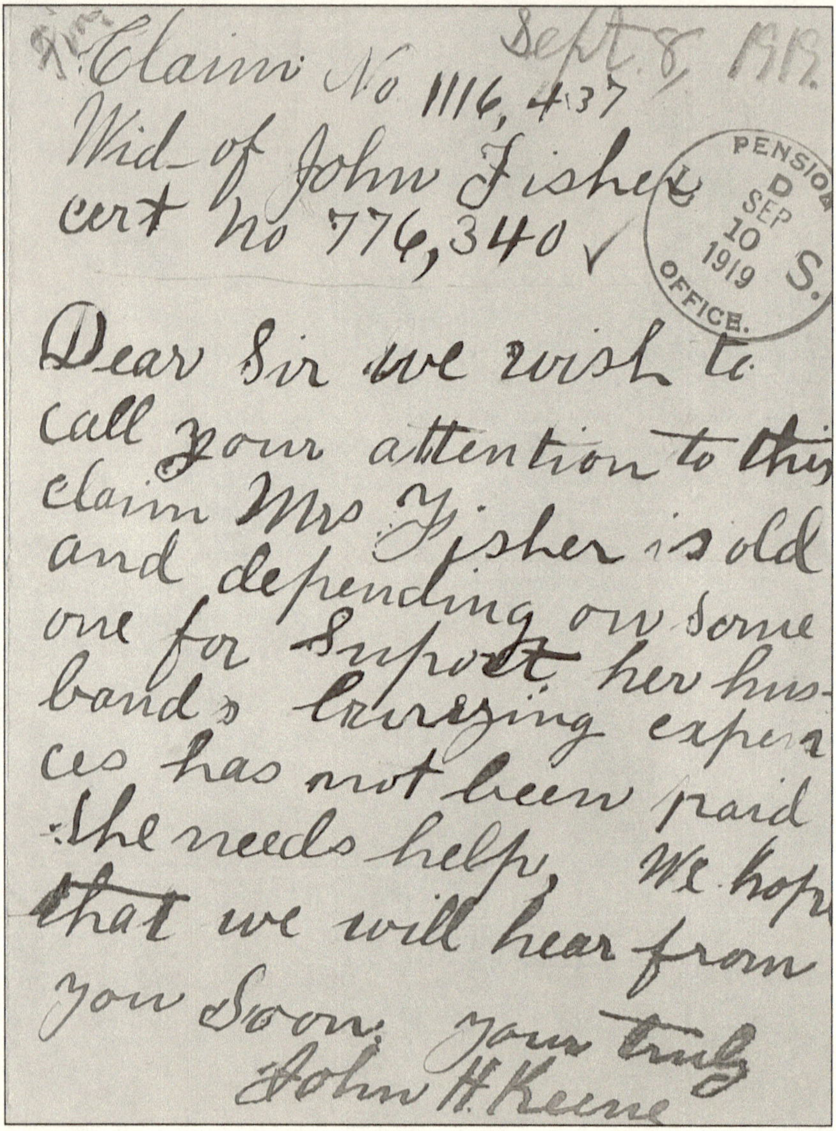

Claim No 1116,437   Sept. 8, AR.

Wid_ of John Fisher

cert no 776,340 ✓

PENSION
D
SEP
10
1919
OFFICE.
S.

Dear Sir we wish to
call your attention to this
claim Mrs Fisher is old
and depending on some
one for Suport her hus-
band's lirizing expen-
ces has not been paid
-She needs help, We hope
that we will hear from
you Soon, your truly
John H. Keene

Letter 2 – John Keene widow's pension letter

292

owned or claimed by Wm Shorter, Sr., and then around with the original courses of said Dashiell's land: and binding with the above named lands of Levin's Ross land a lot owned by William W. Mace to the County road, and with said County road to the place of beginning, and containing one hundred acres of land, more or less, being a part & parcel of land called "Partridge Regulation"; or by what other name or names it may be called — the said described land being a part of the tract of land purchased by the said Edwin Dashiell of James A. Stewart and wife and conveyed to him by deed bearing date the fourth day of February in the year of our Lord eighteen hundred and fifty four, and now, of record among the Land Records for said County, in the Clerk's Office in Liber F. J. H. No. 3, folio 493 and 494 &c. Witness our hands and seals:

Edwin Dashiell (Seal)

Test: Saml. F. Smith.   Ellen L. Dashiell (Seal)

State of Maryland, Dorchester County, to wit: I hereby certify, that on this 12th day of January in the year of our Lord one thousand eight hundred and sixty six, before the subscriber, one of the Justices of the Peace of the State of Maryland in and for said County, personally appeared Edwin Dashiell and Ellen L. Dashiell, his wife, and did each acknowledge the aforegoing deed to be their respective act. Saml. F. Smith, J.P.

Charles Keene. } Be it remembered and it is hereby certified that the following deed to } was received and recorded on the 18th day of January, Anno Domini Fannie C. Dyer } 1866, to wit: THIS DEED, made this fifth day of December, New Page } in the year eighteen hundred and sixty five, by us Fannie C. Dyer and Ann Page of Dorchester County, in the State of Maryland, Witnesseth: that in consideration of the sum of one thousand dollars, we the said Fannie C. Dyer and Ann Page, do grant in fee simple, unto Charles Keene (negro) of said County and State, all that lot or parcel of ground situated in Church Creek District in said Dorchester County and State of Maryland, containing seventy three acres, more or less, and lying between the lands known as Will's Truck or Neals Beach, and formerly owned by the late Henry Page, whereon the said Charles Keene now resides, Witness our hands and seals,

Test:
B. H. Marrington.   Fanny C. Dyer (Seal)
H. T. Winterbottom.   Ann Page (Seal)

State of Maryland, Dorchester County, to wit: I hereby certify, that on this fifth day of December in the year eighteen hundred and sixty five, before the subscriber, a Justice of the Peace of the State of Maryland in and for Dorchester County, personally appeared Fannie C. Dyer and Ann Page, and acknowledged the aforegoing deed to be their respective act. H. T. Winterbottom.

Deed 1 Rev. Charles Keene 1865 land transfer deed

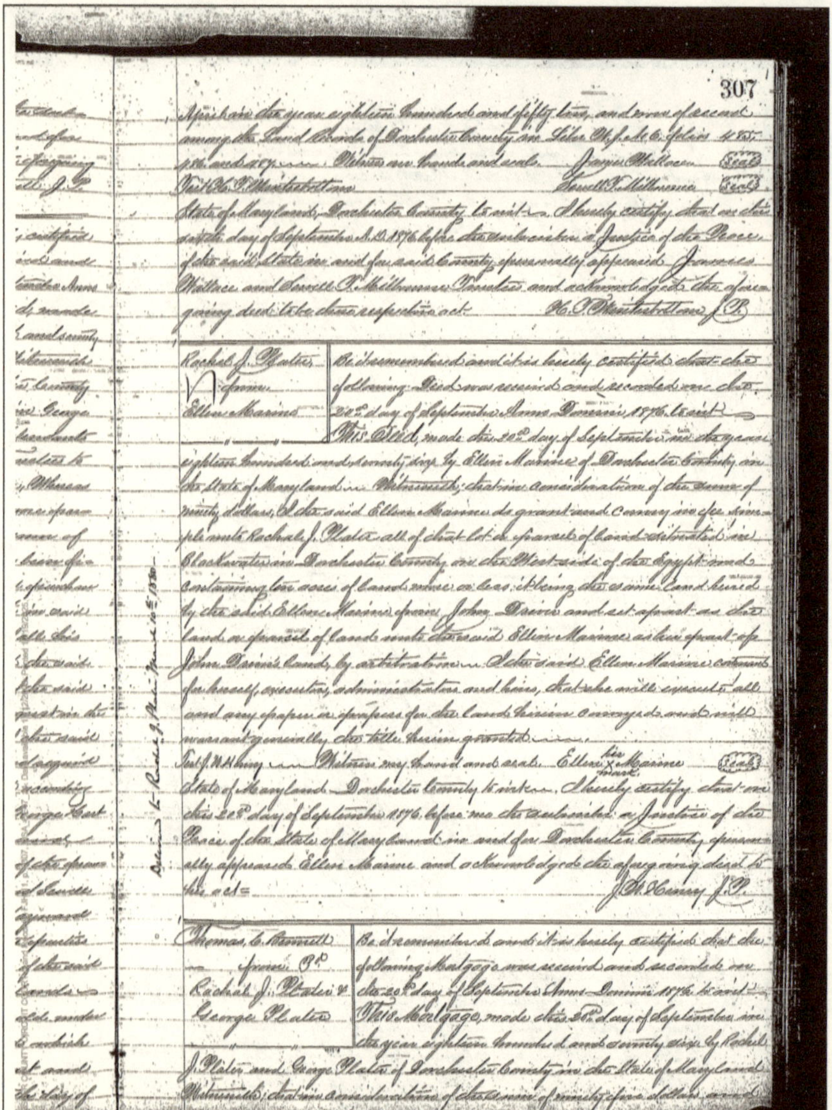

307

April in the year eighteen hundred and fifty [illegible], and now of record among the Land Records of Dorchester County in Liber [illegible] folios 485 486 and 487 — Witness our hands and seals. James Wallace (Seal)
Test H. [illegible] Seweell [illegible] (Seal)

State of Maryland, Dorchester County to wit — I hereby certify that on this sixth day of September A.D. 1876 before the subscriber a Justice of the Peace of the said State in and for said County personally appeared James Wallace and Sewell [illegible] Trustees and acknowledged the foregoing deed to be their respective act. H. [illegible] J.P.

Rachel J. Plater from Ellen Marine

Be it remembered and it is hereby certified that the following Deed was received and recorded on the 20th day of September Anno Domini 1876. to wit —

This Deed, made this 20th day of September in the year eighteen hundred and seventy six by Ellen Marine of Dorchester County in the State of Maryland — Witnesseth; that in consideration of the sum of ninety dollars, I the said Ellen Marine do grant and convey in fee simple unto Rachel J. Plater all of that lot or parcel of land situated in Blackwater in Dorchester County on the West side of the Egypt road containing ten acres of land more or less, it being the same land hired by the said Ellen Marine from John Davis and set apart as the land or parcel of land unto the said Ellen Marine as her part of John Davis's land, by arbitration — I the said Ellen Marine covenant for herself, executors, administrators and heirs, that she will execute all and any papers or purposes for the land herein conveyed and will warrant generally the title herein granted —

Test J. W. Henry — Witness my hand and seal. Ellen (her x mark) Marine (Seal)

State of Maryland Dorchester County to wit — I hereby certify that on this 20th day of September 1876 before me the subscriber a Justice of the Peace of the State of Maryland in and for Dorchester County personally appeared Ellen Marine and acknowledged the aforegoing deed to be her act. J. W. Henry J.P.

Thomas C. Bennett from Rachel J. Plater & George Plater

Be it remembered and it is hereby certified that the following Mortgage was received and recorded on the 20th day of September Anno Domini 1876 to wit —

This Mortgage, made this 20th day of September in the year eighteen hundred and seventy six by Rachel J. Plater and George Plater of Dorchester County in the State of Maryland Witnesseth; that in consideration of the sum of ninety five dollars and

Deed 2 Rachel Plater 1876 land transfer deed

[Ed. Form, No. 3.]

TEACHER'S MONTHLY SCHOOL REPORT

For the Month of _March_ ...., 186*9*

☞ To contain one entire calendar month, and to be forwarded as soon as possible after the close of the month.
☞ A School under the distinct control of one Teacher, or a Teacher with one Assistant, is to be reported as one School.

[Answers placed here.]

Name of your School?	_Beverly School_
Is it a Day or Night School?	_Day_
When did your present session commence?	_March_
Is your School supported by an Educational Society?	_Yes_
Is your School supported wholly by local School Board?,	_Yes_
Is your School supported in part by local School Board?,	_No_
Is your School supported wholly by the Freedmen?	_No_
Is your School supported in part by the Freedmen?	_Yes_
Have you had Bureau transportation this term?	_Yes_
Who owns the School-building?	_Freedmen_
Is rent paid by the Freedmen's Bureau?	_Yes_
What number of Teachers and Assistants in your School?..	
Total enrolment for the month?†	_55_
Number enrolled last report?	_47_
Number left school this month?	_U_
Number now Scholars this month?	_8_
What is the average attendance?	_89_
Number of Pupils for whom tuition is paid?	_50_
Number of White Pupils?	_0_
Number always present?	_8_
Number always punctual?	_28_
Number over 16 years of age?	_8_
Number in Alphabet?	_9_
Number who spell, and read easy lessons?	_10_
Number in advanced readers?	_45_
Number in Geography?	_7_
Number in Arithmetic?	_45_
Number in higher branches?	_8_
Number in Writing?	_8c_
Number in Needle-work?	_89_
Number free before the war?	_89_
Have you a Sabbath-School?	_No_
Have you an Industrial School?	
State the kind of work done?	

Location (town, county, or district)? _Dorchester Co._
Of what grade? _Junior_
When to close? _July 1_
What Society? _New Eng._
Name of Board or Com.? .... Am't pd. this month?
Name of Board or Com.? .... Am't pd. this month?
Amount paid for this month?
Amount paid for this month? _$60.00_

How much?
White? _1_ Colored? ......
Male? ...... Female? ......

{ Number enrolled last report, by adding new scholars and subtracting those left school, will equal the present total enrolment. }

How many Teachers? ...... How many Pupils? ......
Number of Pupils? ......

☞ To the following questions give exact or approximate answers, prefixing to the latter the word "about."

1. Do you know of any Schools for Refugees or Freedmen not reported to the State Superintendent? .... How many? _Unknown_
2. Give (estimated) whole number of pupils in all such Schools? .... No. of Teachers, ... White, ... Colored, ...
3. Do you know of Sabbath Schools not reported to the State Superintendent? .... How many? ....
4. Give (estimated) whole number of pupils in all such Schools? .... No. of Teachers, ... White, ... Colored, ...
5. State the public sentiment towards Colored Schools, ...
6. How many pupils in your School are members of a Temperance Society? _0_ Name of the Society? ....
Remarks, ...

(Signed) _Mary S. Osbourne_
                                             Teacher.

* Or School Committee, either District, Town, City, County, or State?
† A pupil is not to be reported as enrolled until after five days' attendance.

Freedmen's Bureau Monthly Teacher Report (Mary S. Osbourne)

Church Creek map (circa 1865) showing Beverly School "Colored School 1". Courtesy of Ancestry.com.

Dorchester County Tax Roll

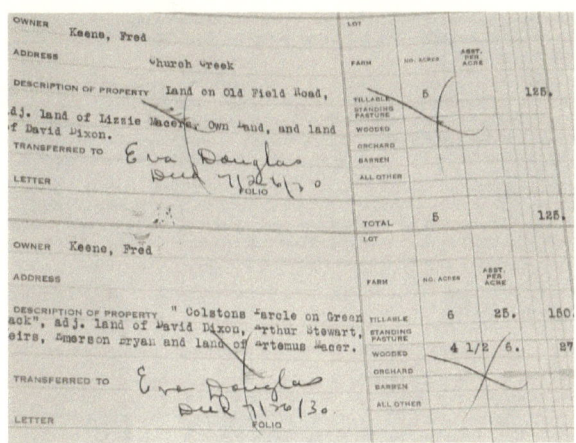

Oldfield Sample Tax Rolls

OBITUARY

JOHN H. KEENE

CHURCH CREEK, MD.
MARCH 30, 1930

JOHN H. KEENE, son of Murray Keene and Amelia (Linthicum) Keene, was born about the year 1850, near Madison, Maryland. At the beginning of the Civil War, he was 11 years of age and had two sisters and six brothers. His oldest brother, George, was killed at the Battle of Petersburgh; and both of his parents died during the War. At the close of the War he was staying with his grandparents

He was now fifteen years of age, and growing strong in both body and mind. There were no schools for Colored People, but young John learned rapidly, and soon became one of the foremost Mathematicians of his time among Colored people. When Colored schools were opened, he was the first Colored person in Dorchester County to receive a regular Teacher's Certificate (in 1872, when he was twenty-two years of age.)

He first taught at Madison, Md., under Dr. James L. Bryan as Supt. of Schools, and received

about Twenty Dollars per month. At that time Colored Schools were open only four months,— but Colored people were anxious to learn, so that during the thirteen years he taught at Madison, about ten pupils finished their Courses of study, and were admitted as Teachers by the Board of Education.

— ### OTHER OCCUPATIONS —

In the Summer Season, when school was closed he farmed and sometimes fired threshing machines. He became interested in Engineering and purchased books on the subject. He was also one of the foremost wrestlers of his time.

In the year 1881, while teaching at Madison, he was married to Miss Annie Chase, daughter of Robert and Sarah Chase, of Vienna, Md. Miss Chase, at that time was sixteen years of age.

He now became interested in Carpentry, purchased a set of carpenter's tools and gradually became skillful in use of same. He built several sail boats, at Madison, one of which was thirty-two feet long and seven feet wide and the fastest boat in the Madison Harbor at that time (Church Creek, Md.)

In the year 1887 he decided to take the school at Oldfield, moved his family there, and five years later (1892) purchased about four acres of ground near the Oldfield Church, from Mrs. Addie C. Boudle, Washington, D. C. Two acres of this lot were later sold to one Josiah Ennals, who never preferred a deed, and at whose death the said two acres were re-purchased by the former owner. The Trustees of the Oldfield School were as follows:- James Macer, Alexander Plater and William Vaughn.

He decided to try farming and on Aug. 6th, 1896, moved upon a farm on the Mapledam Road near the Dixons Chapel Church. At that time the farm belonged to Joseph H. Neal; at present, it belongs to Alfred Mills. After about 16 months of farming he became disgusted and moved back to Oldfield. He taught 2 yrs. at Bucktown, 1897 & '98, 3 yrs. at Church Creek & one at Cross Roads.

During the 13 yrs. he taught at Oldfield, 13 pupils finished their courses of study as Teachers, and were admitted by the Board of Education. Among some of them were the following:- Tomy Vaughn, Many Dixon, Emma Dixon, Mary Jane Macer, Florence G. Macer, John, F. Macer, Rosy E. G. Cromwell, Elnora Vaughn, Martha Dixon, Stella Keene & Geo R. Keene. He taught his last year at Oldfield in 1910, and was placed upon the teachers retired list having taught altogether 34 yrs.

About that time he was converted, during a Revival, while Rev. Angulo was on Church Creek charge, and since then has been a member of the church. Thus for the last 20 yrs., he has lived quietly, farming in Summer as much as he could and doing woodwork and some carpentry whenever able to

In the summer of 1929 he became weaker and began to show signs of infirmities. In December his children were notified and his son came home expecting to take him back to Baltimore. He refused to go stating that his business affairs were not in proper condition. About the middle of February, however he decided to go, and reached Baltimore safely February 24th, 1930. After reaching Baltimore he appeared to rally for sometime, but it was only temporary, and on March 23 became decidedly weaker. Conse-quently it was decided to ...

Page 1 of John Keene's Obituary

Index

H

Haley, Alex 65
Harford County 2
Hargis, Hattie Waters 55
Harriet Tubman Museum and Educational Center 17
Harriet Tubman UGRR Byway 34
Harriet Tubman UGRR Museum 33
Harrisville 10, 34, 35
Harvard University 29
Hayes, John 26
Hayes, Mabel (née St. Clair) 26
Henry family 25, 59, 69
Heritage Weekend 24, 25, 53
Hicks, Moses 29
Hill, Theodore W. 37
Historically Black Colleges and Universities (HBCUs) 13
Howard University 29
Hughes family 27, 52, 59
human trafficking 5, 65
Hurston, Zora Neale 18, 80

I

Indian Wars 37
Indigenous peoples 7, 11
I've Got the Light of Freedom 26
Ivory Coast 76

J

Jackson, Thomas E. 37
James Macer 38
James, Thomas 37
Jarman, William 25
Jenifer Institute ("Colored" School No.1) 48
Johnson-Mansfield, Gloria 49
Johnson, Mary 54
Johnson, Walter 54

Jolley family 70
Jones, Leon H. 62
Jones, Mary C. 62
Jones, Rev. Linda 17
Jones, Roger 72

K

Kane family 59
Keene family 25, 26, 59, 69, 70
Keen, John H. 39
Kennedy, President John F. 26
Kentuck Swamp (Blackwater Refuge) 25
Kiah, Ellen 38
Kiah, William "Bill" 38
King, Charles 37
King Jr, Rev. Dr. Martin Luther 26
Knox Presbyterian Church 21
Kotz, Mary Lyn 28
Kotz, Nick 28
Kowaliga, Alabama 58

L

Lake family 69
land deeds 2, 19
Larson, Kate Clifford 60, 71
LeCompte family 69
Lee, General Robert E. 37
Leonardtown xi
Lexington Market 51
Library of Congress 36
Lincoln, Abraham 50
Lincoln House 53
Linthicum family 21, 34, 59, 69
Lloyd, Leona (née Keene) 29
Lloyd, Martha 29
Lloyd, Ruth 29
Lyttleton. See Littleton

M

N

Endnotes

1 Natalie Hopkinson, *After the Civil War, African-American Veterans Created a Home of Their Own: Unionville.* Smithsonianmag.com. September 2017.

2 Unionville. https://talbothistory.org/collections-research/collections-archives/unionville/

3 Maryland's free communities extend to prior to the Revolutionary War. Intermarried with Native communities.

4 Abolitionist William Still (c1819-1902) was active in abolitionist movement and was called the father of the UGRR. His recorded detailed accounts of the escape from the South maintained the secrecy of those who provided aid to the self-liberation movement. Still's parents were enslaved on Maryland's Eastern Shore before safely arriving in New Jersey in the early 1800s.

5 William Still, *The Underground Rail Road: A Record* (Porter and Coates, 1872).

6 Dorchester County Historical Society.

7 Dorchester County Historical Society. *Historic African American Schools of Dorchester Driving Tour.* www.dorchesterhistory.com

8 Leon Harris. Personal Interview. October 25, 2025.

9 John H. Keene's engraved headstone in the Oldfield Cemetery shows him as the first Black school teacher in Dorchester County. Before arriving at Beverly School, in nearby Madison (formerly Tobacco Stick). He is credited with teaching over a dozen Black students in Oldfield who were among the first to successfully pass the state teacher's examination.

[10] Maryland's Eastern Shore remains a mostly rural region east of the Chesapeake Bay and west of the Atlantic Ocean which shares a border with Virginia to the south, and Delaware to the northeast. Maryland's history and consequence of being the northern most of the southern states that allowed slavery that strategically borders Pennsylvania, Washington DC, Virginia and New Jersey is not inconsequentially relative to being the home of many of the country's preeminent figures: Frederick Douglass, Harriet Tubman, Josiah Henry (of *Uncle Tom's Cabin*), and later Thurgood Marshall.

[11] Baltimore Afro-American. *More people and things.* Elizabeth Bryan birthday. January 16, 1960. P. 4

[12] Brief Local News. The Daily Banner, Cambridge, MD December 21, 1918. P 3

[13] Negro Villages Self-taught and progressive Colored people of Dorchester County. Baltimore Sun. December 5, 1896. P 8.

[14] Vaughn also played for Major League Baseball's Anaheim Angels and New York Mets.

[15] Maurice Vaughn. Personal Interview. October 25, 2025.

[16] The state's oldest HBCU in southern Maryland, Bowie University, has roots with the Freedmen's Bureau Maryland when it began as Baltimore Normal School for Colored Teachers. On the Eastern Shore, the Delaware Conference Academy opened in 1886 and is today known as University of Maryland Eastern Shore.

[17] In Black communities Memorial Day stemmed from Decoration Day, when after the Civil War, families adorned USCT veterans' graves with flowers and memorials.

[18] If Alexander and Susan Ross are siblings, their shared ancestry would be linked to Isaac and Roseann (née Dixon) Ross who lived in both Tobacco Stick and Oldfield, according to 1860 and 1870 census records.

[19] The Henry surname is represented by trustees of several of Oldfield's founding institutions. John J. Henry was a named trustee for the 1869 school deed and William Henry was a named trustee for the 1887 cemetery deed.

[20] A son Alfred Henry Jr. (1939-2017) was a Vietnam War veteran. Nicknamed "Boots," he and his common law wife Darlene Jones were caretakers for his father.

21 Black Veterans Project, in partnership with Yale Law School's Veterans Legal Services Clinic, accessed July 10, 2025, *blackveteransproject.org;* Richard V. Reeves and Sarah Nzau. "Black Americans are much more likely to serve the nation in miliary and civilian roles." Brookings Institute. Aug 2020. *Brookings.edu.*

22 Beverly Stock Club to Winfield Ross. Maryland State Archives (hereafter MSA) CE47_112. Dorchester County Circuit Court. RSM 61. P 600-601

23 William and Ethel Dean are the parents of a noted civil rights leader from Baltimore and state legislator with the Maryland House of Delegates Walter R. Dean Jr. (1934-2015).

24 Old Field Church Creek Community Improvement Association, Inc. (hereafter OFCCCIA) "Message from the President" Our Second Heritage Weekend Celebration September 17-18, 2005. Cambridge, MD. 2

25 "Message from the President"

26 "Among the Freedmen in Maryland No. 3," *Zions Herald and Wesleyan Journal.* (Boston) 37, no. 3. (January 17, 1866): 9. Accessed from Archive.org.

27 "Among the Freedmen in Maryland No. 2," *Zion's Herald and Wesleyan Journal* (Boston) 37, Issue 2 (January 3, 1866): 4. Supporting evidence that the original structure of Oldfield church served as an active school prior to the arrival by teacher, Mary S. Osbourne as described during her initial visit. The current structure was built in 1894.

28 Josiah Parker et als to John A. Fisher. MSA CE47_29. (1893). Accessed from Dorchester County Circuit Court Land Records CL 17, 735-6.

29 John and Jane Fisher to The Trustees of Vaughn Chapel of Beverly. MSA CE47_30. (1894). Assessed from Dorchester County Circuit Court Land Records. CL 18, 398-99.

30 Frederick Douglass Keene Sr is the brother of Ethel Keene, organizer of the Baltimore committee and both are the grandchildren of Oldfield founder, Rev. Charles Keene. Ethel Keene is the grand-mother of Monica R. J. Bland the organizer of the 130th Vaughn Chapel celebration held in 2024.

[31] Baltimore's grassroots community has a history working towards social justice in concert with a coalition of churches. Moore was president of the Friendly Helping Hand Club, the Afro reported in 1956, when they provided 100 inmates at Crownsville State Hospital with personal hygiene provisions, fruit, and baked goods. A coalition of social justice organizations today is represented by Baltimore United.

[32] OFCCCIA. "In Reverence of the Clergy of the Oldfield Community." *Our Second Heritage Weekend Celebration September 17-18, 2005.* (Cambridge, MD, 2005), 4. Former pastors of Vaughn ME Church are listed mostly by initials and surnames as J. Augulo; J.R. Bowden, WC Bowland; J.W. Bowling, Briddell, J.J. Helm; W. E. Hilton; Holden; S. Landford; D. W. Martin; Louis H. Martin; McBride; R. R. McDowell; Charles A Norwood; E. O. Parker; J.R. Purnell; R. H. Slacum and W. C. West.

[33] "In Reverence," 4. Local preachers are listed as Sarah Stafford; William Guy Bryan; J. W. Camper; John Fisher; Dorothy Griffin, George Keene, Julia Stafford; James R. Vaughn; Milton Vaughn, Sr.; Thomas E. Vaughn; William David Vaughn, Sr.; William A. Vaughn; Wilbert James Vaughn. Vaughn M.E.'s first pastor appointed by the conference was Rev. W. E. Hilton of a suburb of Baltimore who lived in New Jersey.

[34] "How to live past 90 Years: 'Never touch a drop,' says matron as she passes 9-decade mark." *Baltimore Afro American.* July 18, 1959. 25. Accessed from *Newspapers.com.*

[35] "How to live past 90," 25.

[36] Among Durham (c 1820- c 1910) and wife Harriet (c 1835-1913)'s known daughters are: Dora Sudler, Anne Camper, Hattie Wilson, and Ada Waters.

[37] The Pinderhughes surname started after James Hughes, the son of Denard and Hester Hughes married Joanna Pinder, the daughter of Charles and Charity Pinder and had children in Rhode Island. Their offspring adopted the conjoined name of Pinderhughes, and later their parents adopted Pinderhughes as their surname. A grandson, William Pinderhughes (1919-72) and his wife Alice were leaders in the Baltimore City school system.

[38] OFCCCIA. "Brief History of Vaughn Chapel Church." *Our Second Heritage Weekend Celebration September 17-18, 2005.* (Cambridge, MD, 2005), 5-6.

39 "Brief History," 5-6.

40 "Brief History," 5-6.

41 OFCCCIA. *Vaughn Chapel 130th Anniversary* Program Cambridge, MD. 26 May 2024.

42 "Vaughn Chapel 130th," 2-3. Earl Stanton was also congratulated grounds and buildings safety and maintenance.

43 "Vaughn Chapel 130th," 2-3.

44 Charles M. Payne, Jr. *I've Got the Light of Freedom: The Organizing Tradition and the Mississippi Freedom Struggle.* His grandmother Rachel (née Plater) Payne of Cambridge in included in the dedication of his book.

45 Joseph Fitzgerald. *The Struggle is Eternal: Gloria Richardson and Black Liberation.* University of Kentucky Press, 2018.

46 Fitzgerald. *"The Struggle"* p 174-75; p 182-83.

47 Herbert J. Gans. "Welfare Activist." *New York Times*, September 4, 1977, Accessed July 2025. Nytimes.com

48 Gans. "Welfare Activist."

49 It appears that the Pinder family who married into the Wiley branch in Rhode Island is an entirely different Wiley family that Calvert Waters of Baltimore married into.

50 Party in Cape May celebrates birthday of Mrs. Olive Waters. The Afro-American. October 11, 1958. P 8.

51 Rev. Bryan's parents, William L. and Elizabeth (née Chester) Bryan, had twelve children. Former OFCCCIA presidents Leven Bryan and Winfield Ross Jr. were his brother and brother-in-law, respectively.

52 William G. Bryan's great grandparents (the Hughes and Pinders) were likely close relatives to Bucktown hero, Denard Hughes, a member of the famed Dover 8 who narrowly evaded capture in Delaware when seeking freedom from enslavement in Maryland with the help of Harriet Tubman.

53 Archaeological Collections in Maryland. Maryland.gov. Accessed October 2025.

54 Bethel A.M.E. Church. Maryland Historical Trust Maryland Inventory of Historic Properties Form. MSA D-591

55 Annual Conference of the Methodist Episcopal Church. Delaware Conference Minutes. July 1880.

56 Historic African American Schools of Dorchester Driving Tour." *Dorchester County Historical Society*, Accessed, June 2025. www.dorchesterhistory.com/services-6.

[57] "9. Malone's Church," Harriet Tubman Underground Railroad Byway, accessed July 10, 2025, https://harriettubmanbyway.org/malones-church/.

[58] Malone's church. Accessed July 2025. *Maloneschurch.com.*

[59] Samuel Linthicum and others to William D. Vaughn and others Trustees. MSA CE 47_22. (1877). Assessed from Dorchester County Circuit Court Land Records CL 10, 13-14.

[60] John A. Fisher and wife to The Trustees of Vaughn Chapel of Beverly in Dorchester County ME Church. MSA CE47_30. (1894). Assessed from Dorchester County Circuit Court Land Records CL 18, 398-99.

[61] Maryland Commission on African American History and Culture. Maryland Historical Trust. "Historic African American Cemetery Project." 2022. *mht.maryland.gov*

[62] Land in the area is mostly small tracts owned by individuals making research of government negotiations acquisitions tedious, if not impossible. The exception is a large tract (8,700 acres) owned by Del-Mar-Va Fur Farms, Inc. that in 1931 was the primary acquisition for what became the Blackwater Nature Reserve. Several state grants were awarded to individuals under the guise of conservation. One program "Rural Legacy" appropriated $128 million during its initial phase in 1998-2002 that appear to have benefited those with political or socio-economic status. "Honoring Black History on National Wildlife Refuges: A Cultural History Tour," *US Fish and Wildlife Service*, February 7, 2022, *fws.gov*

[63] Rosanne Skirble, "Chronic Flooding Threatens Sites Along Harriet Tubman Underground Railroad Byway," *Maryland Matters*, October 11, 2021.

[64] Cemetery records kept by OFCCCIA are unofficial and incomplete.

[65] Camp Stanton was established in Southern Maryland, west of the Patuxent River in 1863 to recruit and train soldiers. Black men from across the state and nearby Virginia fled their enslavers to enlist in the 7th, 9th and 19th USCT infantry.

[66] US Colored Troop veterans were mustered out nearly a year after white soldiers returned home and began collecting their pension. Barriers involving soldier's knowing their date of birth, proof of marriage, access to medical services, and baseless evaluation of the character of witness further delayed or denied applications for invalid and widow's pensions.

[67] OFCCCIA records.

68 1850 Federal Census. Schedule I. Free Inhabitants. District 1. Dorchester Maryland. August 12, 1859.

69 Jeremiah "Jerry" Marine, Durham Clash and John Clash are listed as Beverly School trustees in 1869. Jerry and his wife Mary (née Keene) are buried at Christ Rock United Methodist Church cemetery in Cambridge. A different USCT veteran Jeremiah Marine (c 1838-1864) of the 4th Reg was killed in action. John Clash likely relocated to Baltimore by 1871 according to a deposit record in the Freedmen's Bank. Durham Clash Sr. (1825-c1910) married Rev. William D. Vaughn's sister Harriet and lived in Cambridge.

70 George Plater, this writer's 3rd great grandfather, last appears on the 1880 U.S. Census as a resident of Church Creek at age 62 with his wife Rachel 45; Son George 22 and daughters Cornelia 25, Elizabeth 12, and Ellen S. 10. His neighbors are John and Emily Jolly, William and Mary Hughes and James and Leah Bowley.

71 Debra Holtz, and others. "National Landmarks at Risk. How Rising Seas, Floods, and Wildfires are Threatening the United States' Most Cherished Historic Sites". *Union of Concerned Scientists. eesi.org,* May 2014, 10-12.

72 "Among the Freedmen in Maryland No. 3," *Zions Herald and Wesleyan Journal.* (Boston) 37, no. 3. (January 17, 1866): 9. Accessed from Archive.org.

73 Kay Najiyyah McElvey. *Early Black Dorchester, 1776-1870: A History of the Struggle of African Americans in Dorchester County, Maryland, to Be Free to Make Their Own Choices.* 1991

74 First Annual Report of the Baltimore Association for the Moral and Educational Improvement of the Colored People. November 1865. P 23.

75 Commissioners of Church Creek to Sheldon R. Vickers. MSA CE_47-781. (2002) Assessed from Dorchester County Circuit Court Land Records MLB 727, 356-58.

76 "D-739 Church Creek Black School" Architectural Survey File. Maryland Historical Trust, 2002. *mht.maryland.gov.*

77 Church Creek Black School No 2. *Maryland Historical Trust.* D 739. October 11, 2011.

78 "Among the Freedmen in Maryland No. 3," *Zions Herald and Wesleyan Journal.* (Boston) 37, no. 3. (January 17, 1866): 9. Accessed June 2025 from Archive.org.

[79] Due to Maryland's proximity to Washington DC, Lincoln suspended habeas corpus effectively jailing people with dissenting political views.

[80] American Journal of Education. Henry Barnard, Ed. Office of the American Journal of Education Vol 3. (Hartford): 3.

[81] David Nicky Henry. *Up Pine Street A Pictorial History of the African American Community of Cambridge, Maryland 1884-1951*. Self-published. 2003.

[82] A. M. Foley and Gloria Johnson-Mansfield, *Images of America: Dorchester County* (Arcadia, 2002), 123.

[83] Daniel Orem to Charles Keene and wife MSA CE47_7. (1894). Assessed from Dorchester County Circuit Court Land Records. FJH 7, 480.

[84] *Daniel Orem to Charles Keene.*

[85] "Among the Freedmen in Maryland No. 3," *Zions Herald and Wesleyan Journal.* (Boston) 37, Issue 3 (January 17, 1866): x. Accessed from Archive.org.

[86] "Among the Freedmen in Maryland," *Zions Herald and Wesleyan Journal.* (Boston) 37, Issue. 48 (November 29, 1865): 192. Accessed from Archive.org.

[87] "Among the Freedmen in Maryland No. 3," *Zions Herald and Wesleyan Journal.* (Boston) 37, Issue 3 (January 17, 1866): 9. Accessed from Archive.org.

[88] James Lloyd Hughes (1867-1941) and his wife (the daughter of Charles Pinder and Charity Vaughn) Jennie (1860-1916) died in Rhode Island. They and their children assumed the surname of Pinderhughes.

[89] "Among the Freedmen in Maryland No. 2," *Zions Herald and Wesleyan Journal.* (Boston) 37, Issue 1 (January 3, 1866): 4. Accessed from Archive.org.

[90] "Lincoln House" *The Daily Times.* Salisbury, MD. February 12, 1959. Assessed June 2025. *Newspapers.com*

[91] Kay Najiyyah McElvey. *Early Black Dorchester, 1776-1870: A History of the Struggle of African Americans in Dorchester County, Maryland, to Be Free to Make Their Own Choices.* 1991

[92] "Early Black Dorchester."

[93] Personal interview. *Calmetta Brinkley.* July 2025

[94] "*Calmetta Brinkley*"

[95] Hattie Waters was born and raised in nearby Somerset County and attended Beverly School, according to oral reports. Her husband David H. Hargis was a pastor at Waugh Chapel Church in Cambridge.

[96] "The truth behind Oscarville and the violent removal of Black residents from Forsyth County years before Lake Lanier was built" Gainesville Times. 2022. Updated September 2023. *gainesvilletimes. com*

[97] Beverly Stock Club Charter. Dorchester County Circuit Court. CM 429-4. February 2, 1921. P 89-91.

[98] Charles Keene from Fannie C Dyer and Anne Page. 18 January 1866. MSA CE47-6. Assessed from Dorchester County Circuit Court Land Records. FJH 6. p 292-93.

[99] "Cambridge, MD" *The Afro American* newspaper. 2 May 1924. Pg 12. *Newspapers.com*

[100] Kate Clifford Larson, *Bound for the Promised Land: Harriet Tubman*. New York. (Random House, 2004), 89-90.

[101] Harkless Bowley and wife [Kissiah Jolley] to John F. Henry. 18 January 1866. MSA CE47-28. Assessed from Dorchester County Circuit Court Land Records. CL 16 p 276.

[102] Stock Club Charter. Dorchester County Circuit Court. CM 429-4. February 2, 1921. P 89-91.

[103] Beverly United Stock Club to George Spence. MSA CE47_81. Accessed from Dorchester County Circuit Court Land Records. JFD 27, 431

[104] Beverly United Stock Club to Thomas Ross and wife. MSA CE47_112. March 10, 1947. Accessed from Dorchester County Circuit Court Land Records. RSM 61, 600-02. Five acres of land in the village of "Old Field" on "Old Field Road" for one dollar

[105] Rev. Woolford's genealogy and their family reunion explained

[106] Rodney A. Brooks. *The Rise and Rall of the Freedman's Savings Bank: And Its Lasting Socio-Economic Impact on Black America.* Chicago. (Spiramus Press, 2024).

[107] Genetic genealogy creates family history profiles (biological relationships between or among individuals) by using DNA test results in combination with traditional genealogical methods. By using genealogical DNA testing, genetic genealogy can determine the levels and types of biological relationships between or among individuals, according to the Library of Congress' Research guide. https://guides.loc.gov/genetic-genealogy

108 James A. Plater's paternity is unknown. He is well known for his work within the national NAACP organization.

109 Maryland was one of the original thirteen British America colonies. As colonialism spread, native people defended against the advancement. A series of Anglo-Powhatan wars between 1610-1646 ended with substantial lands claimed by the British.

110 Personal interview. Tyrone Nichols, descendant of Harriet Ross Nichols (c. 1795-c. 1870). November 2025.

111 Personal interview. Dr. Dean Smith, descendant of Harriet Ross Nichols (c. 1795-c. 1870). October 2025.

112 SS Harriet Tubman Named for Woman Abolitionist Goes Down Ways at Portland, Maine. *Baltimore Afro American.* June 10, 1944. P 3

113 Sarah Bradford, *Scenes in the Life of Harriet Tubman* (W. J. Moses, 1869). Accessed via Archives.org.

114 Joyce Stokes Jones and Michel Jones Galvin. *Beyond the Underground: Aunt Harriet, Moses of Her People.* (Sankofa Media, LLC, 2013).

115 Ann Keene's enslavers were likely the planters Roger Jones (1761-c1850) and his wife Sarah (née Woolford) or his parents Captain Roger Jones (1732-1783) planters who also granted land in Church Creek land. April 1779 JHC, vol 1, page 230-31.

116 Nanticoke Historic *Preservation Alliance.* Restorehandsell.org

117 Maryland Department of Transportation. Needs Assessment Maryland African American Context. *www.roads.maryland.gov/OED/African_American_Historic_Needs_Assessment.pdf.* May 2024.

118 Maryland Department of Transportation. Needs Assessment Maryland African American Context. May 2024.

119 George Gerswhin. Porgy and Bess. 1935

120 Presidential Proclamation—Harriet Tubman Underground Railroad National Monument. The White House. March 25, 2013. https://obamawhitehouse.archives.gov

About the Author

Keesha Ha is a former journalist and retired community college professor. A native of Baltimore, she has traced her family's roots to several of Maryland's plantations and free Black communities. A genealogist and supporter of Black Lives Matter, she continues to research untold histories, including the impact of Johns Hopkins medical studies on Black families. She currently lives in Southern California with her wife Rowan and son Broderick Patterson Jr. This is Ha's first book.

www.ingramcontent.com/pod-product-compliance
Lightning Source LLC
Chambersburg PA
CBHW020738130626
46554CB00006B/2040